GOD'S REFUGEE

GOD'S REFUGEE

The Story of a Lost Boy Pastor

REV. JOHN CHOL DAAU AND
LILLY SANDERS UBBENS

© 2015, Rev. John Chol Daau and Lilly Sanders Ubbens

All rights reserved. No part of this publication may be reproduced, stored in a retrieval system, or transmitted in any form or by any means--electronic, mechanical, photo-copying, recording, or otherwise--without the prior written permission of the publisher. The only exception is brief quotations in printed reviews. For information, please address Hartline Literary Agency; 123 Queenston Drive; Pittsburgh, Pennsylvania 15235.

ISBN-13: 9781530213252
ISBN-10: 1530213258

For John's mother and uncle:
Tabitha Nyaluak Madior and Paul Aluong Kuer.

MANY THANKS

There were so many faithful brothers and sisters who made this story and its telling possible. We, John and Lilly, would like to thank all our friends at Hartline Literary Press, Daystar University, Trinity School for Ministry, Good Shepherd Academy and Good Shepherd College and Seminary, and to the members of their Board of Trustees.

Special thanks goes to all John's colleagues and students over the years, who were with him in and out of the refugee camps – thank-you for your inspiring faith.

We are thankful for all the love and Generous support from our families; Robert, Sara, Jerree, Matthew, Evan, Inga, Tabitha, Joseph, and Paul. We lovingly remember John's uncle, Elijah, and Lilly's mother, Ramona, two lights in heaven. Most especially, John would like to thank his wife Sarah and their handsome sons Abraham, Isaac, and Jacob for richly blessing his life. Lilly is deeply grateful to her husband Bo and their beautiful children Lydia and Joshua.

And to every reader and friend who supported us along the way: thank you! "Taste and see that the Lord is good; blessed is the one who takes refuge in him," Psalm 34:8.

AUTHORS' NOTE

For years the Jieng people have been referred to as "Dinka." This name is not in their language but was assigned to them by foreigners who misunderstand their language, and it became commonly used. Although Dinka is widely accepted, in this book, we decided to use the original word, "Jieng."

PREFACE

This story is based on the life of the Rev. John Chol Daau, whom I met at seminary and liked immediately. He was soft-spoken, friendly, and always curious. Never failing to ask a steady stream of questions, he loved to learn about people, places, and culture. We became good friends.

In time, I learned something of John's story, how he escaped death on more than one occasion and how he found life. I glimpsed something special in his words, in his tone, and in his spirit. There was a certain strength, the kind of strength which comes from years of deep reliance on a strong God. I wanted to learn more, and what I learned, I wanted to share with others.

I learned John's story over the course of many interviews, informal conversations, and times of prayer together. The more John shared, the more I became captivated by his life. The images of John as a young boy burning down shrines are forever seared into my mind. I recorded the majority of our times together and transcribed them into written form. These transcriptions were the clay of this book which I molded and shaped into a narrative. Many of the words you read are John's exact words, but some of them are mine as well. John provided the broad strokes. I gave shade and highlights. The more we thought, prayed, and shared together, the more I wrote and reflected, the clear dividing line between who was speaking--what is from John and what is from

Lilly--began to fade somewhat. This is, however, a true story. It was written by Lilly and lived by John. The events of John's life have not been changed. They tell the story of an ordinary boy and an extraordinary God.

The war in Sudan is a complex and terrible war whose causes are cultural, political, historical, economic, ethnic, and spiritual. This story focuses on the spiritual as seen through the eyes of one man and told to one woman, a woman who lives in another culture quite distant from the events. Needless to say, it is biased. We have focused on certain things to the exclusion of others. There are many other stories to be told, but the one before you is my friend John's.

And yet, as John told me time and again, John's story is not just about John. "If you tell them anything, Lilly, tell them what Jesus has done." For that reason, this book is also the story of God as told through his people. It is the story of the God who rescues and saves. It echoes of Moses and the Israelites narrowly escaping the waters, of David taking down Goliath, and of Jesus tearing down the tables in the temple. It is a story of biblical proportions and, as with all the stories of the Bible, it reaches its height and discovers its depth with the one who gives the story meaning--Jesus the Word Incarnate. That Word, spoken thousands of years ago, is the Word that was spoken to John and his brothers and sisters in Sudan. It is the same Word that is spoken to us, no matter who or where we are. It is the same Word that speaks to us in this particular moment, no matter where the moment may fall, "I have come so that you may have life and have it to the full" (Jn 10:10).

God has a peculiar way of revealing his greatness in small things, and in John's words, "Now is the time for small things." This story is of humble and small origins, but in it you will glimpse something of the greatness and goodness of God and find everlasting strength that comes from sure and steady faith in him.

Chapter One
THEY'RE COMING FOR US

The sun was rising over the village of Baping, gold and pink in the pale morning light. Rolling over on my mat, in the small corner of our *tukul*, my eyes fluttered awake. Father had left to attend the cattle and my mother, Tabitha, was gathering the morning washing. The hearth was warm and kindled by a fragrant breeze from the open doorway. Neighbors were calling, the birds sang, all the familiar sounds of our village life mingled together. I heard Joseph snoring softly and poked him awake with my toe. For breakfast, we drank milk from a hollow gourd while chatting as young boys do. We always enjoyed a few frivolous moments before a hard day at the cattle camp. Outside, our rooster crowed, and we knew the cows would soon gather to pasture. It was time to begin our work. The smile on Mother's face lingered as she stood outside our compound waving goodbye to us. The wet clothing in her strong hands dripped onto the earth. The sun warmed the village as we walked to the camp with the other boys and started on our daily chore of gathering the cows. We were laughing and talking as we sang to them, swinging our long shepherd sticks.

At once the earth trembled, and the cows ran mad. I dropped my stick and swirled around to find Joseph. I heard an explosion and saw earth bursting upward and outward. Bombs were falling and the ground was shaking. I fell to my knees to cover myself, but more bombs came. I struggled in the dirt, too afraid to get up, but knowing I could not stay where I was for the earth might swallow me whole. Shaken, I pulled myself up to see a hostile Northern soldier appear only a few yards from me. He pointed a gun at a nearby man, a leader in my cattle camp, a man I called uncle. Blood squirted from his head, and he fell to the ground in a limp heap. An idea triggered in my brain. The rumors were true–the North was invading. I began running wildly toward home, screaming for Joseph, but when I saw the soldiers with their artillery coming toward me, I turned around. They were in front and behind, shooting at everyone in sight. Trapped, I stood frozen. I tried to cry out, but no words came. I tried again, but it was as if my tongue was paralyzed, no sound could come. Cattle camp leaders dropped to the ground, blood gushing out of them. An older boy grabbed my arm, pulling me along. I heard the soldiers yelling at us. They wanted to get me, destroy me. They were pursuing us with all their power. I started running with all my strength. The boys from cattle camp were on my left and right, everyone running. The sounds of gunshots, screams, and cattle dropping to the ground followed. I could only run faster. I ran until my knees and heart ached, until there was no wind in me.

We made our way deep into the forest, slowing our pace, no longer able to keep running. My head was throbbing, and I worried I might collapse. I turned to look behind me, but I could no longer see Baping. We were well past the outskirts of our village. My thoughts ran back to mother. I wanted to run back to find her. What had happened to Joseph? He would need me. I called out, my breath heaving, "Where is Joseph?" No one heard me over their own shouting and cries. I doubled over, resting my hands on my knees and gasped for air. I looked around, pausing for the first time. I saw mostly boys from the cattle camps. There were a few young girls and women along with them. Where were their fathers and uncles? Where was Elijah? It was strange to be in the forest, which had always been a still, peaceful place to go and dream. Now, it was filled with noise and human wreckage. I felt myself being pushed forward, but I could scarcely move. Someone was leading me forward. We had no time to waste.

"They are coming for us!" a young girl yelled. The fear in her voice reverberated, cutting through the crowd and confusion, jolting us to action. "They are coming!" I knew the soldiers would get me. The thought was chilling. I didn't see how I could continue, but the boys took off again running, and I dragged myself along with them. As we ran, we called out to each other, "Have you seen my mother?" "Did you see my father?" "Yes, I saw him. He was shot." When we could no longer run, we fell to the ground, taking stock of our wounds and broken limbs.

Our numbers increased--more people with blood and dirt matted to their bodies. I tried to gather more information about the attack. No one knew who had survived. I considered turning back, but our new arrivals informed us there was nothing to return to. Our village was gone, obliterated. There was nothing left, and we would surely die if we went back that way.

"The soldiers are still after us," the new arrivals told the others. "They won't stop." I realized then we were being hunted, the way our uncles hunted wild animals, the way we spent hours searching for a lost calf, never stopping until it was found. They were searching for us and wouldn't stop until we were killed. Our only option was to run toward the River Nile. For the first time, I felt so tired. There was part of me that wanted to lie beside the wounded others and sleep, but I knew what our choices were: run or die.

We ran through the day, and the night passed quickly. We fell asleep in seconds; we were so exhausted. My head merely hit the forest ground, and I was asleep. Other nights and days passed as well. We continued to walk and run.

Were we mourning for our families, for our village, and our shared life together? No, not yet. We had no time, nor physical strength to mourn our losses. Our thoughts were of food, safety, and water. We ate leaves and roots from the ground. We were accustomed to sleeping outside in the cattle camps. Shelter we could forego, but we desperately needed water, and there was no stream or river. I stuck close to a few of my camp friends. One little boy of my group, perhaps four years old, was snatched by a leopard in the night and eaten. I was so exhausted I didn't even hear the screams. Several others, especially the younger and weaker ones, were also eaten by wild animals. I watched as several boys and a few women and girls sat down in the forest and surrendered to death. Most of the elderly had already given up and were left behind to die in the forest. Thirst, exhaustion, and starvation attacked us with a force more powerful than the hostile soldiers with their guns and took as many lives. It appeared to me that some of my companions' bodies were shattering from thirst. Their skin looked like broken glass. I saw many of these same boys drink their own urine out of sheer desperation, but we kept going because we knew our attackers still pursued us, never relenting.

My heart was not yet broken. I had no strength left over for grief after running, hiding, and scavenging for food. I didn't pray much, for I couldn't form the words. My breath and steps became like prayers, each one crying out to God. In my head I felt a continual dull ache. I put everything I had, every thought and physical act, into escaping, running day and night. Only at night, when I lay on the hard grass, my body stiff from pain and hunger, that my thoughts wandered to my mother, brother, and father, wondering if they were alive. "Please Jesus, don't let them surrender and die. Don't let them sit down in the woods to sleep forever." I wondered if Joseph had found something to eat, and if Elijah had gotten away. I recalled each one of their faces. I cried myself to sleep and woke in the morning to a fearful, almost maddening hunger, but I kept going. I couldn't think very clearly, but I was certain that I didn't want to sit down to die like the others.

We hid and ran in the wilderness for four months. Other groups from surrounding villages who had been forced from their homes trekked longer. Massive numbers of Sudanese refugees reached the Ethiopian border. We were met by the Ethiopian government and UN refugee agencies. We were shuttled to large camps, the largest of which, took over 50,000 people. We were mostly young boys who had escaped from the cattle camps. The boys I was with were not all from Baping. I didn't know where many of them came from, but I assumed they came from surrounding villages that had been attacked. They had also fled and joined with others in the forest. The UN officials and Ethiopian government trucked us to different camps located in the Ethiopian wilderness. The scene was a chaotic blur. Young boys hobbled along like old men. I collapsed on the ground with the others. I was vaguely aware of a strong official picking me up and lifting me into the back of a truck. I was amazed at how he lifted me with such ease. My body was so much lighter. I felt my bones pressing against my flesh. I wasn't sure where they were taking me, but I hoped only for water and food. As I lay in the truck, the sun pelted me, blurring my vision, and my thoughts became a mantra: "I didn't die, I didn't die." It was a miracle, one of the many I had witnessed.

Chapter Two
GOD'S GOOD REPLACEMENT

Everyone hoped this pregnancy would be different. No one hoped this more than my mother, Tabitha. This is why she came to the North. She left the only home she knew, our small corner of the world, the village we called Baping. Traveling for days by foot, she finally reached the industrial city of Khartoum. The smells and shouts of the big city overwhelmed her. She never knew such a life with so much noise existed. When she arrived, her brother Elijah and his wife met her. Her feet were so swollen from the last stages of pregnancy and exhaustion, and they carried her home on a stretcher. It was my father's Daau, idea that she go to Khartoum for her safety and, of course, for the baby's. She could stay with Uncle Elijah who worked in the factory, and he would take care of her. They both agreed that it would be better for her there. There was greater access to hospitals, for all the hospitals in the South were crumbling. It was the first of many sacrifices she would make for me.

One long, civil war and years of economic and political oppression had taken their toll on Southern Sudan. We were cut off from the prosperity of the North. The infrastructure of the South, its schools and hospitals, had disintegrated. There wasn't much to help a baby in the South, especially if there were complications as there had been the last time. My family all remembered the last pregnancy and the baby that had come and gone. At the beginning of her long and strenuous labor, it appeared there might once again be complications, and she could not bear to lose another child. She felt the same panic and pain in her belly that tore through the rest of her body. She was in the hospital for many days. Along with her fear, the pain grew greater with time. No one knew what the problem was or how to help. It seemed that she was doomed to repeat what happened before. She closed her eyes, and the haunting image of her last baby placed in a small grave returned to her. "No," she whispered, "not again."

Slowly, one by one, the room started to fill with women. Distant cousins, sisters, and friends surrounded her until she was encircled in her hospital bed. From the outside hall you could hear the chorus of comforting words and murmurs. Mother prayed in every way she knew how. She prayed to the gods of her ancestors, snakes and trees, gods that my people had worshiped for centuries. She even prayed to Jesus, the strange God Elijah always spoke of.

The labor was difficult, marked by her sweat and cries. Everyone eagerly yearned for it to be over and for a healthy baby to be born. Then suddenly something gave way and their prayers were answered. I was born strong and vigorous, crying like a healthy baby, and to mother's great joy, I was a boy! A boy was cause to celebrate. Most Jieng women hope their first child is a boy to carry on the family line. Hopefully, a girl follows to obtain a dowry for the family. Mother's first baby, the one who had died, had also been a boy. She had desperately desired that she would be given another boy, and her wish was granted. The great sacrifice of her long journey was well worth it. Mother held me in her arms and whispered to me, "My son. You are my great compensation."

Before I was named John, I was given another name, "Chol Makeyn" meaning "compensation" or "replacement." The family agreed that I was a compensation for the sadness of losing the first baby--God's good replacement. At my mother's hospital bed, Uncle Elijah declared, "God has restored what we lost and turned our devastation to joy." Everyone agreed that God must have heard the women's moans and cries! And so, I was given another name, "Madioor," meaning the Son of the Women, because everyone--family, friends, nurses, doctors, and neighbors--had heard the circle of women's prayers and cries. I became Madioor, Son of the Women, to everyone who knew me.

Aunts, uncles, cousins, and friends all came to see this new baby boy. They held and cooed to him, singing "Chol Makeyn," the one who paid the debt, the one who is precious to us. This expression endured for years to come. Around my village, my family and clan addressed me, "Hey Madioor Chol Makeyn, you have paid the debt."

I was a fussy, crying baby. Mother broke down from being kept up all night with my perpetual tears. She sang to me, coaxing me to sleep, but I only slept for quick naps during the day and never at night. My auntie remarked that she had never seen so fussy a child. As the crying continued, my family began to suspect that something was wrong. Tabitha feared I had health problems. "This baby was supposed to be different," she thought. "Didn't Elijah say that this baby was God's good replacement and wasn't Elijah someone who understood the things of God?"

There were only two strong Christians in my clan, Elijah and Johnson. Elijah was my mother's brother and Johnson was his cousin. Elijah and Johnson were friends, not simply because of blood, but also because they shared the same faith in the God they called Jesus. For most in our family, that faith was unknown and strange. Elijah and Johnson were the real teachers, the ones who made their faith known by their participation in church.

Their evangelistic efforts often landed them in jail. They were the ones who stayed up late into the night, after the supper had been served, and talked about the Bible and Jesus, *Nhialic*, God of Heaven. Nhialic was our one true God. For centuries we believed he existed hidden in the sky, but Johnson and Elijah talked of him in a new way. It was as if they knew him, as if he was a friend of theirs. Their Jesus had made Nhialic known, no longer hidden from us, and they spoke of him as if he were their very own brother.

Johnson came to investigate the matter of the crying *Chol Makeyn*, the one who had paid the debt. He had been working long hours in the factory and had not yet received the time off to see his new relative. He had heard the report, "Your cousin has given birth to a boy! A compensation, but he cries through the night and will not be at peace." It was in the early afternoon when he called, and I was dozing after a night of unrest. Tabitha lay beside me exhausted, having hardly slept since my birth. Her face tired and her appearance unkempt. It was obvious that the hard work of motherhood was taking its toll.

"Tabitha, what have you brought?" asked Johnson. His voice was comforting, his face shining. "I understand that you have brought us a boy who will not stop his crying." Johnson carried his New Testament. It was a nearly complete translation from English to the Jieng language, a rare treasure to find and even rarer to own. It was dangerous to have a Bible. "May I see your little boy?" Tabitha mustered a smile and led him over to my mat. "I heard that you can't stop crying," he whispered. "You need only to be woken up." He smiled down on me, his very presence like a benediction.

"There is no use," Tabitha said, shaking her head. I have tried everything. "He will simply go back to crying. I'm afraid for him, that something is wrong."

Johnson shook his head no and patted Tabitha on the arm, trying to reassure her. He walked over to my mat and knelt beside me. Gazing down at me, he raised his Bible and held it over my eyes.

"Hey, boy," he whispered, "instead of crying you will proclaim this Word. Wake up and look at the book!"

Mother tells me that my eyes immediately opened, and I reached for the book. I grabbed it and held on with a weak, tiny fist. Uncle Johnson and Mother stared. It was as if something miraculous had occurred, and yet it was seemingly ordinary, a baby simply reaching for a book. My crying ceased.

"I will leave the book with you," said Johnson, "for you seem to like it."

Mother had never seen me look so peaceful and alert. She was thankful and relieved. Before Johnson left, he laid his hands on us and said a blessing for me.

"Your boy should talk a lot about this Word rather than cry at night. This Word will be his cry," he reassured her. "God will keep him, and one day he will be a true compensator."

Mother nodded in agreement, although not fully comprehending what he meant. She couldn't read or write, and the Bible was foreign to her. She touched it lightly, tracing the words with her finger. She placed it near me and hoped that Johnson's words would come true.

The family agreed that "Chol" needed another name. A name that would describe what had occurred. What they had witnessed was not simply a little baby gripping a story with a message, but rather, as an infant, I had inherited an object of power. To my family, it was as if the book was a force in itself, and it changed the way they saw me. They seemed to think that I somehow shared the book's strength. This made me different. Everyone agreed I was to have a special life. Elijah suggested the name John, not after my Uncle Johnson, but after John the Baptist, another one who could not stop talking about the book, the one, who in the wilderness, called the people to prepare God's way.

From that day onward I was reportedly a relatively happy baby. I loved to be held by strangers and was often passed around. Mother was proud to hand me to friends, family, and neighbors. She always said that I seemed to love everybody and was loved by many. She didn't worry about me. She noticed that I rarely looked for her or cried for her. I did not cause trouble with other children or fight over toys. She thought that I had an unusual gift for getting along with others, and she knew that it was a part of Johnson's blessing. She kept the book by my bedside and would often hold it up for me to see.

Mother stayed in the North for some time while I grew strong and healthy. She was unsure of Uncle Elijah's God and didn't know what Father would think. She had been raised in the ancient system of worshiping our ancestral deities. She prayed to our families' *jak* or spirit.[1] The *jak* could be ancestors, or at other times, they were trees or rivers, bulls or snakes, but they were worshiped and passed down through our families. The way of the *jak* was how Mother was raised, and she always called on them for help in trouble. These things were basic to our way of life and could not simply be forgotten, but she often went along with Elijah's religious talk and activity to show him her respect.

When Elijah began to take me to church, she didn't mind or object. Since Elijah played an important part in the church service

---

[1] The *jak* (plural) or *jok* (singular) are spirits, usually ancestors with sacrificial cults. They can take the form of animals, such as snakes and bulls, or nature, such as trees and rivers. They are divinities that are worshiped and passed down through the family. In this system of religion, sacrifices and offerings are continually made to appease or gain the favor of the *jak*.

and needed to have his hands free, he often gave me to a relative to hold during the worship. Elijah was a skilled preacher and leader. People looked to him for guidance, and at this time, we were in desperate need of guidance. Our church met secretly in a deserted warehouse. Christianity in Khartoum was all but outlawed, and we weren't able to come together regularly. But when we did meet, we prayed and praised God for hours. The adults had learned no real rules as far as worship went. They sang, gave testimony, heard Elijah preach, and shared God's word together. Sometimes we shared a sacred silence as the Spirit moved among us.

In the late seventies, when Elijah was meeting with his people, there was talk of civil war and the political situation was precarious. In the North the hostility toward Southerners was palpable, and the spiritual climate was uncertain. In 1964 the Christian missionaries had been expelled from the country. The government began to strip the country of all signs of Christianity. There was a brief period of peace between the North and South in the seventies, during which the missionaries were allowed back, but now the atmosphere was changing again. The Northern government was moving toward an enforced Islamic state, and this only served to harden the bitterness between the North and South. In 1983, Islamic law (*Sharia*) was instituted throughout Sudan. Christian worship services were forbidden. Going to church was dangerous, and the majority of churches went underground.

Elijah had been threatened by the government for speaking about the God of heaven and earth. He was thrown in jail, but days later, was unexpectedly freed. Elijah's faith was tried and proved to be true. He often stated that Jesus came to him in the jail. Many of the Christians in the North grew fearful. Our small band was no different. Elijah heard that Christian leaders were being imprisoned, publicly whipped, or secretly executed. These Christians were accused of promoting disunity in the country and forced to swear an oath of allegiance to Islam. Elijah remembered the war that had ended not long before, and rumors of a new war intensified. He had lived through the first war, knew the signs, and began to gather his family together. He knew it would not be safe to be a Southerner and stay in the North. He was certain that it would not be safe to be a Christian anywhere, but he knew our best hope was in the South, and so, we began to prepare to move back to Baping.

Chapter Three
BOY OF THE DRUM

In the center of my village, a slaughtered elephant lay dying. It was a beautiful creature with long, ivory tusks. Baping's spiritual leader, the *tiet*, had lured the elephant from the bush to display his power. The animal came, innocent and unassuming. We watched as the *tiet* stroked the animal's ears, whispering to it, and then quickly with no warning, drove the spear deep into the animal's flesh, blood spilling over the marble gray skin. Defenseless, the creature lay on its side as the *tiet* slowly brought it to death. As he finished the job, he called on the *jak* for favor, to be pleased with our sacrifice. This set the crowd afire with noise, they moaned along with him. Some threw their hands into the air in exaltation. They all pleaded for the *Jak's* favor to rest on them. A shiver moved down my spine. I looked up at Elijah, my eyes filled with questions. His face was a hard mask, but I could see anger and shame seething behind the surface as he gazed at the crowd.

"I don't understand," I whispered to him. "What are they doing?"

He rested his hand on my shoulder. "Our village does not yet know the ways of Christ." He looked down at me, his eyes comforting, yet I still didn't understand what I had witnessed. Why did the people kill this elephant, and why did it bring about such frenzy among them. I couldn't take my eyes off the dying creature.

The crowd seemed so pleased with its death and the ugly, powerful display of the *tiet*. Elijah crouched down beside me, resting on his heels, so that we were at the same level "This is our task," he said. He waved to the crowd. "They do not know. We must be the ones to tell them." We looked at each other. He was serious, and so was I. We made an unspoken agreement. Later the animal would be used for tokens and meat. Its hooves and horns would adorn the many shrines that were in the doorways and homes of our village. But before they took it down, they left it to die in the center of the village as a testament to the power, the lordship of the *jak*, who had for centuries demanded our worship and sacrifices.

When I first moved back to Baping, I was still a little fellow, and although it was entirely different from what I had known, I loved the change! I was reunited with my father and extended family, and I was free to run about barefoot with the other boys. I distinctly remember how they loved to pronounce my name. They found it an interesting novelty. No one in my village was named John. It was not a traditional Jieng name, but a Christian one. "Is 'John' from the North? Are you from a strange town?" they asked. In the cattle camps, the young boys would run after the cows in the pasture, and my friends would call the name over and over, "Hey John, hey John." [2] One boy would say to another, pointing over at me, "Hey, see that boy? He is called John." When the rebel leader of the Sudanese People's Liberation Army, Dr. John Garang, became a popular hero, many asked if I was named after him. I knew, however, that I was named after a great saint of the Bible which, as Johnson had prophesied, was a book I could

---

2 Under the direction of their fathers and uncles, Jieng boys and young men take care of the cattle, learning to be herdsmen and participants in Jieng society and culture.

not stop talking about.[3] The book set something in motion in my life, something that grew with time.

There was no church in Baping. Elijah was the only Christian, and he took it upon himself to teach me. Of all the Bible stories, I was most fascinated by my namesake, John the Baptist. Elijah described to me the wild man who called the people to repent. He often taught me with songs and showed me how to beat the drum along with them. Our lessons under the trees could go on for hours. One teaching, the other learning, but you would always find us singing,

> This man who was like a crazy man,
> He was preaching and talking loud.
> He put on his belt.
> He wore one cloth and ate honey.
> He cried in the desert.
> He didn't live with the people,
> But he told them to turn away from their sins.

This song led me to imagine a wild-eyed man and I laughed and laughed. "Why does he eat honey?" I asked Elijah one day. "Does he not drink milk? We drink milk."

"He eats the honey because he was living in the wilderness and that was all he had," said Elijah.

"Why does he tell the people to turn away from sins? Where are the sins we have to turn away from?"

Elijah described the evil in the world, the violence he had witnessed in Khartoum and the hate in people's hearts. "John the Baptist was an interesting man," Elijah continued. "His parents were very old, and his father was a priest."

---

[3] Formed in 1983, the Sudanese People's Liberation Army waged a guerilla war to liberate Southern Sudan from the Northern Government.

"What is a priest?" I asked.

"We have no name for it, but it is similar to the *tiet*. Zechariah was a *tiet* for Jesus."[4]

"But, my Father is not a *tiet*," I protested.

Elijah smiled. "That is probably a good thing, John. One should want only to be a *tiet* for Christ."

The next time I went to the cattle camp, I took note of how the other boys treated each other. I saw a big brother strike his little brother with the big stick we used to steer cows. When I returned from the cattle camp that day, I stopped by Elijah's compound.

"Uncle, there were many boys who were having sins today."

Elijah smiled, clearly amused by my frankness. "What sins did you see?"

I told him of the big brother that treated his little brother poorly and beat him with a stick. I recounted how some other boys were calling each other names and bragging. I talked animatedly to my uncle, describing in detail the sins I saw at camp. I was excited, at last, to finally understand what sin was.

"Now you know what John the Baptist was calling the people to turn away from," Elijah said.

"Oh yes," said I proudly. "Now I see the sins the people are having."

Elijah nodded gravely. "You will see even more with time."

One Sunday morning Elijah came to fetch me. "Chol Makeyn, today is Sunday, the Lord's Day. We must begin to tell the people that Nhialic has been made known in Jesus." He pointed to my drum, which I quickly grabbed before we headed to the central square of Baping.

---

4 "Nhialic" or the "one in the above" is the Jieng term for supreme divinity or one God. He is inscrutable and unknown. Here, Elijah appropriates the term to a Christian context. In this way Nhialic means God made known in Christ.

Men and women were milling about, starting their morning chores. Elijah stood erect and quiet under a few large trees which provided shade from the morning sun. He opened his New Testament (we still did not have fully translated Bible) and began to read, "In the beginning was the Word and the Word was with God and the Word was God..." He paused for a moment, letting the words seize people's attention. A curious few dropped their morning work and made their way over to him. Elijah continued reading loudly so that all could hear. Others saw a small crowd gathering around him and came to see what was happening. Women and children sat down and listened in front, while the men stood back, listening intently. Elijah looked at their wondering faces and began to pray, "God of Heaven and Earth, we thank you that you are no longer hidden, but have come to us in the form of your Son Jesus to save the world which you loved so much."

At these words, the people exchanged confused glances. One man placed his hands over his ears as if hearing a great noise. He was completely baffled. A woman whispered to another, "Have the pressures of living in the North changed him for the worst?" There were murmurs, whispers of confusion. The villagers circled around him, listening, looking at one another in disbelief. "Is he crazy? Has he gone mad?" they asked.

"Elijah, what are you doing?" an elder in the village asked for all to hear.

"I am worshiping God," he replied.

"We worship the gods of our grandfathers. Who do you worship?"

"I worship the God of heaven, Jesus Christ. He alone atones for sins."

They shook their heads, shocked by what he was saying. None of their gods atoned for sins. Rather, they required that you make atonement. All of their gods demanded sacrifices--bulls, goats--and there were certain gods that few would speak of that even demanded human sacrifice. This man, Elijah, however, was telling them of the God who sacrificed himself for them. It was strange. "What kind of God would sacrifice himself?" they asked.

Many of them didn't like it and shunned Elijah. They didn't understand what heaven was, at least not in the sense that Elijah was describing it. They considered heaven to be the sky, the place where Nhilaic, the one in the above, lived in seclusion, removed from his creation. They believed that when they died, they went to be with their ancestors, but they had no idea where or what that was. Elijah was now telling them there was a place to go called heaven, and that there was a man there too, and he was like their ancestors, but greater. It was a dangerous notion that shook their beliefs. Elijah had become a crazy man.

Elijah came back the next Sunday. He knew his task would take time, and he would not let the difficulties of his first attempt stop him. This time only a cluster of people came to listen to his words. Although it was a wild idea, there was a small few that accepted the news at once with joy. As a young child, it was hard for me to understand the great relief they must have felt after a lifetime of being forced to sacrifice to the gods. They encountered, for the first time, a God who wanted nothing except their devotion, and that there was a place to go when they died. My people had witnessed death for centuries, and now, after death, we could go on living in this place called heaven.[5] In heaven, there would be rejoicing, reunion, and laughter with the people we had lost to war, hunger, or disease.

---

5 The reality of heaven holds great significance for Jieng Christians. They have lived through centuries of warfare and lost friends and family members. The gift of eternal life is an answer to their devastation. Among Jieng theologians, there is no consensus as to what heaven is, how it is defined, and how it is understood.

I was only nine years old, but I helped Elijah in the worship and that is how I got the nickname, "Boy of the Drum," because I loved to beat the drum with all my strength. It had a pulse and rhythm, like a great river current running through me, and it so aptly expressed the joy I felt worshiping God and watching my people turn to him. I knew that people were talking about us, but if Elijah wasn't embarrassed, then neither was I. In time, beneath that tree, a small church was formed. It was modest at first, perhaps five people, but it was the beginning of something. As it was in the days of John the Baptist, people once again couldn't quit talking about a crazy man who stood in the center square of Baping calling people to turn from their sins and draw near to God.

Chapter Four
ELIJAH'S GOD

Sitting next to my uncle, Aluong, one afternoon, I noticed his color had turned gray. The blood on his nose had dried and caked around his nostrils, but he no longer seemed to notice. "Uncle, what can I fetch you? Would you like some milk or water?"

He looked at me with glazed eyes and lifted his hand to wave me away, but even that small gesture seemed too much for him. His diarrhea was constant, and he had a steady flow of blood from his nose. He was fitful at night and never slept. He shifted listlessly on the braided mat Mother made for him. Streams of light flooded our *tukul* creating dark shadows on his still body. He closed his eyes. I prayed Elijah's God would heal him.

Later that afternoon, after playing with the other boys in the Baping courtyard, I waited for Elijah outside our *tukul*. Elijah approached with his usual determined gait, a broad smile on his face. He was on his way to visit the villagers. I dropped my game of sticks and grabbed my drum. Wasting no time, Elijah began our lesson from yesterday, "How did Jesus teach us to pray, Madioor?" he asked.

"Our Father, Who art in Heaven, hallowed be the name," I began, reciting the Lord's Prayer as I hopped along beside him. He listened to my recitation and nodded when I was finished. He was pleased with how I was progressing, and I always took the time to memorize the verses he taught me. He walked briskly, forcing me to keep pace with his giant strides. He placed his steady hand on my shoulder as we walked. We had many people to see. Nearly every day, Elijah visited *tukul* after *tukul*, praying for people and teaching God's word. There was no priest in our village and very few leaders. It was up to us to fill the gap.

"Uncle, why are you always in such a hurry? People laugh at you behind your back. 'There goes crazy, Elijah,' they say 'always running about, never standing still.'"

Uncle chuckled. "I am in such a hurry, because there is so much work to be done."

His smile faded, and he became lost in his thoughts. We knew our village was like a hot and thirsty man at the edge of an unknown river, who must decide whether or not he will drink.

I looked up at him, squinting in the mid-afternoon sun, trying to make sense of his words. He read my puzzled expression and laughed, his rich voice bubbling out. "What I mean, nephew, is that many have heard the message of Christ and have believed, and now they are all watching, waiting to see if it is true, or if these Christians," he trailed off and smiled to himself, "myself and the rest of us, really are crazy. So, let them laugh, Chol Makeyen. They laugh because their hearts are torn, and that is why we are in a hurry. We have so many hearts to reach."

We stopped at a small dwelling. Elijah filled the doorway, and I stood behind him. They welcomed us and we made ourselves comfortable on the living room mats. Some men and women had gathered to hear Elijah speak. He placed his New Testament in front of him and spread his hands over the pages to smooth their creases. His was the only Scriptures our village owned, and it had to be treated with care. He was silent for a moment, filled with the enormity of his task. His eyes scanned the pages of the great book, and I could tell he was praying.

"Jesus teaches us how to pray in this way," he began to read from his New Testament, "Our Father who art in heaven, hallowed be thy name."

He stopped reading, seeing the confusion on their faces. He was silent for a few moments, giving them time to weigh his words.

"What does it mean to be in heaven?" the man of the household asked. By going first, he allowed room for the others to come out with their questions and concerns as well.

"Heaven is the place where God is," said Elijah. He raised his hand to the sky. "It means to be up, with Nhialic, the one true God, made known in Jesus Christ."

"Is that where our ancestors are?" another asked. An important question. We had always believed we would be united with our ancestors, and honoring their memories was an important part of our culture.

"No it is where Jesus, our God is. He is our Great Ancestor, along with Abraham, Isaac, and Jacob and the Christians who went before us. He is in Heaven where there are no tears, pain, or suffering. Where he rules over all, but he is also right here." Elijah placed his hand on his chest. "He lives inside you. His Spirit is forever connected to your spirit. He is here with us now."

"You mean we are with him right now?" a young man asked.

"Oh yes," said Elijah. As he talked, his joy, his passionate energy, began to fill the room. But there was something else as well, someone else. The Spirit of God was entering our village, our doorways, and our hearts. God could be perceived. He was palpable. "He is here with us now," said Elijah. He turned through the withered pages of his New Testament and began to read.

"Where two or more are gathered together in my name, so I will be also," Elijah looked up from his book, his eyes shining. He could feel the effects of his teaching taking hold. "Not only this, but Jesus comes and makes his home with you. He never leaves you." He thumbed through his pages, driven by the dawn of their understanding.

"Ah, yes. Here it is. This is what Jesus says, 'If anyone loves me, he will obey my teaching. My Father will love him, and we will come to him and make our home with him.'"

The room was hushed as the Spirit of God worked inside their souls. They thought for some time and then had more questions for Elijah. The afternoon ebbed and flowed with questions, answers, scripture verses, and more questions, puzzlement and dawning understanding. They could not stop talking about this new God, and they had so many questions.

"Is it okay to still talk to the *jak*?"

"Is Jesus always listening to us, and where does he live?"

"Can we eat the meat of animals that have been sacrificed to the evil spirits?"

The sun passed beyond the trees and still we talked on and on.

Back at home, I pressed a cool, damp cloth to Aluong's nose to gently remove the blood, making him grimace with pain. "Elijah is coming and he will pray for you," I said, hoping to encourage him. He slumped back on his mat and nodded, a slight look of relief spread across his face. Six nights out of the week he was sleepless, but on Sunday, Elijah came to pray, asking Jesus for peace and mercy. Uncle often felt a little better after those prayers. I settled him on his mat so that he would be comfortable. His eyes closed and he looked almost peaceful. I offered a silent prayer on his behalf. "Lord, Jesus, please come bless my uncle and family." How I longed for Uncle, Mother, and Father, for my entire family to give up the *Jak* and turn to Jesus.

When Elijah came that night for the family dinner, we gathered by our kitchen hearth, sitting cross-legged on our mats as we ate the evening meal. Our family *tukul* was similar to many others in our village. It was a small, circular room in which we ate and slept. There was another larger room for our cattle. This is where my father spent most of his time. My family was unique in that Father had only one wife and only two children. We were unlike the many other Jieng families in which a man had two or three wives and several children. Although we were different, ours was a happy family.

That evening, everyone fell upon their food, but Elijah prayed quietly before he began to eat Mother's meal. Mother and Father paid him no attention. Long ago they had decided to ignore Elijah's strange customs. I helped Aluong eat his supper, slowly bringing it to his mouth as he swallowed what he could. I got the strange sense that although he was physically present, his body hobbling along, his spirit had died somewhere along the way.

After dinner Elijah and I brought him into our small family room where I knew we would remain for the rest of the evening. Elijah helped him lie down and then crouched beside him, studying Aluong to see how his illness was progressing. His expression was grave, for he could see that death was coming, and he was deeply troubled. Placing his large hands on Aluong's shrinking frame, he began to pray in his usual earnest way. He closed his eyes and lines formed along his forehead. He prayed with total concentration. "Jesus Christ, Lord of heaven and earth, we ask you to heal this man."

The words hung in the air, seeming to fall away and never penetrating Aluong's heart. His prayer stopped and he seemed defeated. Aluong lay helpless on his mat, looking up at Elijah with watery, bloodshot eyes. I hoped that he had at least found comfort.

Mother, Father, and a few neighbors came to join us. They sat against the wall, watching silently, not participating, just observing. Now and then they talked casually among themselves.

Elijah and his words meant nothing to them. After his prayer, Elijah turned to them. Sweat formed on his brow, and his eyes glinted with a hint of sharpness in the fading evening sun. "How many sacrifices have been made on Aluong's behalf?" he asked, addressing the family.

I could hear the edge of anger in his voice. They shifted in their seats, hesitating. Father looked away. Elijah was a forceful man, and they knew he disapproved of animal sacrifice.

Mother finally broke the silence. "More than fifteen chickens, seventeen goats, and four big bulls," she said.

It was a fortune. These animals were our livelihood, and these sacrifices came at great cost. We had gone without many things, trying to gain the goodwill of the spirits around us. My family was desperate to save our beloved Uncle Aluong.

"The *tiet* came recently," Mother said. "He thought that perhaps another spirit is angered and that one more bull must be sacrificed."

I shivered at the thought of the old witch doctor and his steady stream of sacrifices to the gods. Would my uncle be another victim of the old spiritual order? Would there be another senseless death on our hands?

Mother sighed deeply and looked resigned. I could feel her frustration. She knew it would cost the family, and we wondered where we would find another bull. We had already given all we had.

Elijah slowly shook his head in frustration. "There is no need," he said, his voice a mere whisper. "Tabitha, listen to me as your brother. Aluong must turn to Jesus and be baptized. Let the church come and pray for him."

The room fell silent. My parents frowned, but they were at least considering it. It was a frightening thought, and it came with a terrifying risk. What if they did as Elijah suggested and the *jak* became further enraged? What might then happen to Aluong? Surely, he would die, and how could they spit in the face of everything the elders taught them? But then again, nothing had worked so far, and what if Elijah was right?

"I think we should try," said a frail voice from the corner.

At once, everyone in the room turned toward Aluong. He was nearly asleep, broken down with fatigue, but his words changed everything in an instant. "I think we should go with Elijah," he spoke again, his words final.

Mother put her head in her hands in distress. Our neighbors gasped collectively. Elijah smiled in triumph. I gazed at my uncle slumped in the corner, dried blood on his face and an excitement swelled inside me, like the sun rising over our village, and for the first time, I felt hope.

Aluong was too physically weak to attend a church service, so the church came to him. Elijah planned it so that Aluong could receive prayer from Bishop Nathaniel Garang who was visiting Baping on his tour of the villages of Southern Sudan.[6] Bishop Nathaniel and Elijah, followed by Joseph and myself, gathered together with one hundred Christians. We processed toward Aluong's compound, singing and praying for him. I was in front, beating my drum. I felt so confident, so sure that God would do something for Aluong. I was relieved that my family had made this surrender.

As we processed, many neighbors of the old spiritual order lined the street and watched with fearful eyes. They could not believe what we were doing. My friends, boys from the cattle camps, were looking at me as if I were a stranger to them. There were several who called to us, warning us to stop our foolishness.

---

6 Bishop Nathaniel Garang was a Bishop of the Diocese of Bor. He led a revival, baptizing many thousand throughout Southern Sudan.

"Don't anger the gods," a village elder shouted sternly. "You will regret this. The gods will war in anger against you and your people," he said.

"Listen to him," an older woman said, stepping forward from the throng. "We are afraid for you." Her forehead was creased with worry, and she threw her hands out in a desperate gesture to stop us.

One of Uncle's neighbors who had generously offered one of his bulls for Aluong's healing stood by scoffing and making jokes at our expense as we passed. To him our procession was a silly amusement. He called out to the crowd with a sneer on his lips, "These Christians have gone mad! Let it be known that if Aluong is healed, I will be named Daniel." He meant that if Aluong received healing from the Christian God, he too, would turn to Jesus, be baptized and adopt a Christian name. I paid no attention to his sarcasm; I was only full of hope for my uncle.

We circled the compound several times, praying and making music. Aluong, still a young man in his early forties, was dragged from his bed and carried out on a sheet. He seemed dazed, seeing all the people and all the ceremony on his behalf. He was weak and pale, his body limp. He looked up at the Bishop and Elijah with pleading eyes as they prayed for him, laying hands on him, asking God to heal him and bless his life.

A young woman in our group gently handed him a rustic cross made from fallen tree branches. Moved by her empathy, he clutched it against his chest as if it were a precious gift. He was struck by the way we loved him and had come together for him. Aluong was deeply touched. He closed his eyes and tears slowly ran down his cheeks. We Christians circled around, stretching our hands out toward him, praying both silently and aloud on his behalf.

"I know I am going to die," Aluong whispered to the crowd. "I have no life left, but the little life I have, I give to Jesus."

"Aluong, would you like to be baptized in the name of the Father, Son, and Holy Spirit?" Bishop Nathaniel asked. Aluong, still holding his cross, reached out his frail hands toward the heavens as if he were embracing a long lost friend and nodded yes.

"When we baptize new Christians," Bishop Nathaniel continued, "we ask them to choose a name of others who were Christians before us. Would you like to choose a Christian name?"

Aluong considered the Bishop's words. "Were there any Christians who were terribly bad?" he asked.

"Yes," the bishop answered, "St. Paul."

"I need that name," Aluong said.

On that day my uncle was given new life in Jesus and became Paul. After my Uncle's baptism, there was another baptism. The scoffing neighbor, humbled by what he had witnessed, became a new man in Jesus, known as Daniel. The church was growing in strength.

That evening we destroyed our family shrine. Mother and Father decided at once that we must turn away from the *jak* and embrace Jesus. This meant the old ways had to burn to the ground. Joseph and I ran about our home, collecting the old, sacred objects. Teeth, horns, skins, and feathers had been added to the shrine our family had created over the years. It was a shabby structure, a mere pile of animal remains. We lugged it from our *tukul* out into the open air. In the fading afternoon light, it no longer seemed so menacing and powerful. There was still a large group of us, and we were exuberant from the events of the day. Peaceful and at rest, Paul watched us from a mat on the ground. We circled the shrine a dozen times, calling out in prayer.

"Jesus, you are here with us," Elijah proclaimed. "Praise be to Jesus, who conquers the evil *jak*. Look at you now evil *jak!* You may no longer rob or torture us. Jesus has defeated you!"

Elijah raised a burning stick in the air and threw it at the shrine. It hissed and popped with a loud shrieking "waaah," and then at once the shrine was ablaze. A shadowy smoke seethed from the fire and we cheered in victory. "Yes, Jesus, you are victorious over evil," I cheered over the sounds of crackling fire. There were shouts and whoops of delight as we praised God for his power and might. I began beating my drum and we broke out in joyful, carefree dancing.

The morning after Uncle Paul's baptism, he awoke and called to me. I saw instantly that he was different. His eyes were less bloodshot. He sat upright, rubbing his nose. "Look at my nose, nephew, and tell me if it is bleeding?"

I examined him and confirmed that the blood was gone. He straightened up in his mat, touching his nose in disbelief. I went and got him some milk to drink which he gulped down. I then found some fruit which he ate ravenously. He began drinking and eating with great vigor. He slept through the night and sat upright during the day. I was fetching him food constantly, but we were both excited by the change. In two weeks time, he called to me.

"I think I would like to eat a chicken, Chol Makeyn. Can you go and find me one?" At once, I ran from the house to find a chicken. It was a very unusual request. Chicken was not something we often ate in Baping.

"Madioor, where are you going?" a lady neighbor called to me, wondering why I was racing from our *tukul* toward the pastures.

"I am going to find my uncle a chicken," I called to her over my shoulder.

She was surprised. His desire for meat was a sign that he was healing. She pointed to where she thought some might be, and I headed in that direction down the mud path.

After that, Uncle Paul ate a chicken nearly every day. Before sunrise a cock would crow and my uncle would nudge me in my sleep. I would get up and Uncle Paul would be waiting for me. "In that direction," he said, pointing. "There is a chicken. Will you go get that chicken for me?"

He ate chicken and milk and soon became strong. The word began to spread of Uncle Paul's healing, and that he was sleeping, eating, and smiling. The people of Baping would drop by to see Uncle Paul, bringing a chicken for him to eat. They had heard of his new appetite. Many sat by his mat, just staring at him completely amazed. He looked like a new person. He was youthful and healthy, no longer old beyond his years. His countenance had changed. We had never seen him that way. He was friendly and generous, telling lots of jokes. The God, Jesus, had healed him and this God was able to do what all the *tiet* and all the sacrifices could not do.

"So, you didn't sacrifice any more bulls?" a man who lived nearby asked, trying to make sense of what he saw before him.

"No, I turned to Jesus Christ and he healed my body completely. He is like a *tiet*, but much better and stronger. You should turn to him," said Paul.

The man, clearly startled, sat and thought in concentration. "Aluong," he said at last. "I think I know what happened to you. Perhaps, there is another *jok* who is secretly behind this, perhaps masquerading as something else. This has to be the work of the *jak*."

"Not true," Paul said, slapping his hand firmly on the ground, as if to dismiss such a foolish idea. "I know what has happened to me. I was there and I lived through it all. So many *tiets* were consulted, animals sacrificed, and only the prayers of the Christians worked. There is life in Jesus Christ alone. That is it." His words were final.

Uncle Paul was a loved and respected member of our community. So many villagers had rallied behind him, making sacrifices to the *jak* on his behalf. Now here he was saying such crazy things and never shutting up about the God, Jesus, who had healed him. Talk about Uncle Paul spread all over the village. Everyone wondered what had happened to him. Several believed that Paul had gone mad and could no longer be trusted. Others reasoned that Paul's healing had to be a trick of the *jak*. Uncle believed that his sickness was a result of his reverence for the *jak*, and that once he turned to Jesus to be baptized, the curse had been broken. There were many who began to believe that what happened to Aluong was the work of the greatest *tiet* our village had known and that Jesus was the God of gods. The thirsty man was beginning to drink.

One day, as I was playing under the trees with the boys from the cattle camp, one of my uncles came for me. "Chol Makeyn, your mother is delivering and has been in pain for two days. We need you!"

In my culture, we call all our aunts "Mother." I was immediately afraid. I did not understand how women made babies, and I knew that there was something dangerous and grown up about the situation. Because I was scared, I didn't want to go with my uncle, but I followed him in obedience. As I walked behind him, I kept turning to watch the boys play soccer and wanted to run back and join them.

I heard adult voices, rising and falling, before I entered the compound. They were huddled over my aunt and arguing among themselves. She was drenched in sweat, her face colorless with fear. Her husband sat beside her, holding her hand. He was looking at her intently, searching her face for any sign of change. Her eyes were closed from the pain. She was no longer laboring, but dozing off and on. The pain had overwhelmed her, and she was giving up.

"We have to call for the *tiet*," her husband said, his voice commanding. "We can't just let her die."

A few others in the room nodded, agreeing with him, but one of my aunts spoke up. "We no longer do such things. We've turned to Jesus now. What would Elijah and the Christians say?"

Uncle's jaw clenched and his face darkened. He formed a fist with his hand and slammed it against the thrush wall. The entire *tukul* seemed to quake with his anger. I took a step back and huddled by the door. "I don't care what they say! This is my wife and I will not set the *jak* against her."

One of my aunts cried out, "No, Jesus is our God now. We can't betray him."

One or two nodded with her in agreement, but the others appeared conflicted. The confusion was etched in their faces. Uncle turned and looked at me, as if seeing me for the first time.

"Nephew," he said, placing his large hands on my small shoulders. "We have to save her! Tell them to send for the *tiet!*"

He was shaking me, wanting some kind of answer. I could feel the fear welling up inside of me. Uncle was so big and strong, but more than that, my faith was being tested. What if we didn't send for the *tiet* and my mother died? Uncle would be without a wife and their children motherless. For a moment I could not think beyond the fear, which banged in my head louder than any drum. Then I remembered what I had seen with my own eyes--no *tiet* healed Uncle Paul. Only the Lord Jesus Christ did that, and the truth came to me with the force of a charging bull.

"Uncle," I said, "no *Tiet* can heal her. Only Jesus Christ can save our mother."

My uncle winced at the words and I could see how torn he was. He released me. Kneeling by his wife, he rested his head on her shoulder and whispered something to her. Her sister came and knelt beside him. The tension and the growing heat of the room made it hard to breathe. She placed her hands on Uncle's shoulders and spoke softly to him. Uncle hung his head. He was done fighting.

"Chol Makeyn is right," she said. "Let's pray to Jesus." She turned to me, "Chol Makeyn, you must be the one to pray. We follow Jesus now and no longer make sacrifices. Come Chol Makeyn, pray to Jesus for us."

She bowed her head and took my poor uncle's hand. They both kneeled beside their wife and sister. Soon everyone bowed their heads and many were on their knees. I stood very erect, horribly embarrassed and scared. All the boldness and certainty was gone. I uttered a quick, earnest prayer. "Dear God, let my mother deliver."

I turned and ran out of the door, too scared to look back. I ran and ran, heading for the boys playing soccer in the field. When I saw them, I just kept running. Could they understand what had just occurred? I ran until I found a solitary place on the outskirts of my village and stayed there for a long time lying in the grass. I prayed quietly thinking about what had happened and what Elijah had told me, "They are all watching now, waiting to see if this Jesus can be trusted."

I could feel that we were at the edge of something great, but I knew they were all waiting and watching to see if what we believed was true. "Oh, Jesus," I prayed, "please let this prayer be answered."

That evening when I arrived at our family dwelling, Mother was waiting for me at our door. When I saw the joy in her face, my heart beat faster.

"Chol Makeyn," she said, taking hold of my hands. "You prayed for your mother. They were here earlier to tell you that she safely delivered a baby. She is at home resting. I am proud of you, son."

Relief flooded my entire body and in an instant I was exhausted. Mother drew me toward her in a hug and I exhaled, thankful. Tomorrow, I thought, after the cattle camps, I would like to go and see the little baby. I didn't quite realize at the time how significant this miracle was. I only knew what little teaching Elijah had given me, and that his God was true. I could pray to Jesus for things and he would answer. He could be trusted, and so, I began this work of following Jesus. I was without sophistication, acting in response to what I had seen with my own eyes, the trusting eyes of a child. I wondered if the others would hear of the miracle.

That Sunday morning I would have my answer. I ran from my family dwelling with my drum in hand. The sun was a small sliver in the blue dawn light. I heard the rooster crow as I made my way to the big trees. My neighbor stood in her doorway, watching me, and cradling a sleeping infant.

"Get ready," I yelled for all to hear. "It's time for church."

I banged a short rhythm on my drum to alert them. We Christians had church every Sunday, but nobody knew at what time. For the most part, we didn't have watches, and if we did, we wouldn't have bothered to check them. When the sun rose and the roosters crowed, I knew it was time to start getting ready to go meet the others at the big trees. Elijah was already there, a tall figure, and as was his custom, dressed in a western suit. He was holding his Bible under his arm and talking with three young people. As the head pastor and church founder, he was always there and usually the first to arrive so he could greet the people. At other times, Joseph and I would get there first. The little group was talking animatedly. As I approached, Elijah turned toward me.

"Chol Makeyn, I see you have brought your drum. Are you ready to worship the Lord today?"

The green tamarind trees, shining in the sunlight, covered our heads, creating perfect shade and a natural canopy. He looked behind me to see the cowherds in the distance, taking the cattle out to graze.

"The cows are ready and so are we," he said to the group.

He was smiling and the young people laughed with us. Once the cows were pastured, that meant it was time to start making our way to church. It wasn't far, only at the edge of our village, but still, we took our time getting there. We had no bulletin, no schedule.

As we walked through the village, we saw people outside washing clothes, preparing food, and looking after livestock. Children were playing in the grass and old people were reclining on benches. When they saw us, many quit what they were doing and joined the procession. As the sun grew brighter in the morning sky, more people came outside to greet the day. People called to us, "Hey, sit down and talk for a little."

Elijah always sat and talked when he was invited, and he was known for his eloquence. We visited the homes of church members to remind them, "Hey, we are going to church. Come with us!"

They finished up whatever work they were doing and called to the neighbors, "Elijah is going with his people to church," or "Hey, the church people are already gone. I'm late!"

We began to sing songs and pray to God as we walked along. No one could miss my drum playing. It was a mix of divine worship and the boy in me wanting to make a racket. We stopped and prayed for three sick people, but no one seemed to mind the delay, because this was part of what it meant for us to go to church. I saw Father and Mother, with Uncle Paul and little Joseph, behind me in the throng. Nearly my entire family and clan were there. They had heard of the miracles, and it was like Elijah had said, they were watching and they were now beginning to trust. I banged my drum behind my uncle and our group grew from twenty to thirty to fifty. We formed a mighty procession, walking through Baping on our way to worship.

A young woman came running from her house and flung herself at Elijah's feet, begging him for help. She had heard of the recent miracles, Paul's healing, Mother's safe delivery, and many of her neighbors were turning to Christ. "The *jok* of my house is tormenting me. I want to come with you, but he won't let me and now I am terrified to return. What should I do?"

Still huddled on the ground, she looked up at Elijah. Helping her to her feet, he turned to the others and announced that we would have to stop. We entered this woman's home and collected the teeth, horns, and other sacred artifacts, throwing them into the shrine behind her house. She trembled and was too afraid to touch them. Unable to speak, she could only point to the artifacts. I went through the compound, making sure we had found all the traditional religious relics and then we began our service in the customary way. We circled the house praying, worshiping God and singing. I beat the drum with all the force inside me. We burned the shrine to the ground and danced around the fire. This young woman was fearful, but one of the mothers of our group held her hand and walked with her. We all rejoiced, even the young woman whom we embraced and congratulated. She was crying now, happy to have joined us at last. The *jok* had been defeated. After this, we took her with us to the church. She joined our procession, and we arrived at our tree church as the sun was still rising.

Our worship that morning was guided by the Prayer Book. We had taken turns learning how to use the old book that missionaries had brought years back, but now for the first time, it was truly ours. It had an order for prayers, preaching, and music.

"What do we know about Jesus Christ?" Elijah's voice seemed to quiver with the rising heat of the day. The sweat dripped from his forehead, but he didn't notice. He was seized by the message he had for us. "We know that he is the most powerful God. He is the God of all gods, the one true God. For years we have worshipped the *jak*. We have sacrificed our livelihood, our families, and our food for this evil *jak* with the hope that it would not be angry, that it would have favor on us."

He paused collecting his words and the people were listening intently. An elderly woman stood beside Elijah wringing her hands, she was so troubled in her spirit. Elijah turned to her and then to all of us. "What did the *jak* do for you? He hurt you! He enslaved you, but this is what we now know, the *jak* was weak!" At this, spontaneous cries erupted from all of us. The old woman jumped and threw up her hands in exultation. "It has been defeated, thrown down and cast out, because there is one who is more powerful. He is the only one who can save us from all that is evil!" Pausing for breath, Elijah's countenance changed and he became peaceful, full of tender feeling. "And he loves us, he wants good for us, to bless us in our land, rejoice with Responding to the call, we danced in worship, old and young together. Elijah, clearly tired from preaching for over an hour, leaned over toward me.

"Chol Makeyn, might you share a few words?" He could see that I was shy and nervous. "Don't be afraid, nephew."

I walked to the front with all eyes on me. It was not typical for a young person, much less a child, to speak at public meetings, but Elijah had confidence in me. I felt so mortified to be speaking and wished Elijah would pass me by, but I knew I must be obedient.

"'I am the vine, you are the branches.'" I began to recite one of the many Scripture verses I had memorized. "'If a man remains in me and I in him, he will bear much fruit; apart from me you can do nothing.' Jesus Christ is the true Christ, the only living God and the only God worthy of our worship. He healed my uncle when the *tiet* could not, and he has answered many other prayers."

At this, I sat down. Taking a deep breath, I tried to steady myself. It was a modest beginning. I was always shy to speak in the company of elders, but Elijah wanted me to get accustomed to it.

Others came forward to testify of what God was doing in their lives. Many shared of things they had seen, prayers answered, and the peace of Jesus they had received. We began to sing together.

> The *jok* has been defeated. Jesus has thrown you out, evil *jak*.
> It started right here in Baping and we will tell the people.
> And we will go to the village of Nimule, and we will tell them.
> And we will go to the village of Yambio, and we will them.
> And we will go to all the villages of Bor, and
> we will tell them…

Our singing and praise was so great that morning, I truly believed we would tell the world, starting in the Jieng villages of Southern Sudan. We had come to the edge, thirsty men and women, and we drank from the river of life. Jesus had come to Baping! He had brought new life and joy that could not be held back. We didn't know then that our faith in Jesus would change everything, our lives, our village, and our families. Our new life in Christ threatened hundreds of years of ritual and tradition, and the ancient fabric that once held our village together, was beginning to unravel. Jesus was coming not only with his peace, but with his sword.

Chapter Five

UNRAVELING

I was walking through my village one afternoon, feeling the warm, packed dirt under my feet. Joseph was skipping along in front of me, happy to be done with the cattle camp for the day. Women and children sat in the doorways of their *tukuls* preparing food, sweeping their compounds, and talking to each other. At their entryways were crosses made of tree branches, a symbol of a household's conversion. I greeted them as we passed and stopped to talk with a few mothers from church.

"Can your sons and daughters come out and help us gather wood for our new church?" I asked. They smiled in agreement. The children dropped their work to join us. As we walked toward the bush, Joseph and I picked up a few more friends to help us gather. We talked and joked together. We were excited for our Christian community and to be part of building something together. The Church of Baping, as it had come to be called, was growing. It now had close to seven hundred members and counting; more than half the village had come to Christ. We felt a need to have a cool, safe place to worship long into the evenings. At the edge of our village, we began collecting fallen tree branches and throwing them into piles.

The tamarind trees in Baping, known for their long shade-providing branches, were once considered sacred objects. They were thought to shelter spirits and had been worshiped by certain clans for centuries. One could not cut them down for any purpose. Even using the fallen branches for firewood was forbidden. As we gathered the wood, I thought how amazing it was that something which once frightened us could now be used to glorify God. I looked at the tall slender branches with fresh eyes, and I saw for the first time their grace. They were no longer something to fear.

That evening my family gathered in our compound for a family meal. We were eating and drinking around our hearth. We heard a rustling sound outside our windows, and then it grew louder. What was it? Rising from our meal, Father peered from the doorway of our family *tukul*. His body stiffened with fear. He turned to Mother, "Keep watch over the children," he told her. He straightened himself and stepped outside to greet the men. There were four of them and they were seething mad. Not listening to mother's orders, Joseph and I joined him, and standing behind him, peeked out to see why these angry men were here.

"You and your family are ruining our village. You are blasphemers. You are destroying godly things, going around tearing down our sacred trees. These children have insulted our gods!" The man in front, clearly the leader, pointed at Joseph and me. We were terrified. What if they hurt Father because of something we had done? The man continued to hurl insults at us. "You are teaching our children to do ungodly things. It is shameful, a disgrace."

I recognized him as a leader of our village council. My family clung together in our front yard. Mother was behind Father, with Joseph and I to the right and left of her. We didn't know what these men might do. Would they be moved to violence? They raged for several minutes, and then, quite suddenly, walked off in a fury. Before they left they threw rocks at Father's feet. I flinched. I heard Mother gasp in fear. Father was sweating, but holding himself together. "Go back inside," he said. We gathered together around the table again. Mother held us in her arms. Father sat with his head in his hands, trying to think of how to protect his family. We were all shaken.

Elijah and his family came by that evening to join us in prayer. The men had stopped by his house also, but this wasn't the first time they had come. As the leader, Elijah bore the worst of the intimidation. We had started something in Baping. The transformation of our village was intense and rapid. It was a strange and beautiful time, filled with excitement, but we realized that something had changed in our common life together, something that couldn't be undone. The ancient fabric that held our village together was beginning to unravel. Would there be more "visits"? More insults? Would it get worse?

Days later Joseph and I were playing ball in the village center. Word got out about Elijah's refusal to eat meat sacrificed to idols. The elders, those in positions of power, had gathered together for a late afternoon feast, enjoying the cool of the air, talking and eating together. As Joseph and I were playing, I overheard them discussing Elijah. One man did most of the talking. His voice rose and fell as the group grew more and more excited. Joseph and I stopped what we were doing to listen. Because we were young boys, they paid us no attention.

"These children!" the elder said, "are going wild. How can they have the audacity to profane what is so sacred to us?" I knew instantly what he was talking about. In recent months, groups of young men and women had been meeting together to pray and discuss God's Word. At times, moments of worship and singing would erupt among us. Young women, who were rarely permitted to leave their compounds except for dances and the courting rituals around the fireside, were going outside with greater and greater frequency.[7] They were at church, singing up front so that everyone could see them, and testifying for all to hear. They were dancing at the shrine burn-

---

7 In Jieng culture, young women are encouraged to stay indoors and help with domestic labor. They rarely leave their compounds except for special communal events or gatherings, such as dances or celebrations. Given the dowry system, a young woman's reputation is of vital importance for the social and economic status of the family.

ings and prayer meetings. They gathered with young men around the big trees and stayed there in fellowship. It was unthinkable.

"What is he teaching them?" another man asked with growing intensity. "We never had children go and sit under the trees by themselves. Elijah and his followers are breaking all the rules. He has changed the minds of our children and is destroying our customs."

Joseph looked up at me, afraid. We abandoned our game and ran home. How were we to know that our new life in Jesus could be so threatening?

Even my family felt the pains of division. One evening I walked to my maternal grandmother's house for a family meal. As I entered her hut, the smell of roasting food wafted through the doorway and my stomach churned. I had been working in the cattle camps all day. Grandmother was deep in the *jak*, so I knew the meat had been sacrificed to her snake-god, *Atim*, and I didn't want to eat it. Not having seen me for some time, Grandmother was delighted at my visit. She sprang to her feet to embrace me. As the first son of her daughters, I held a special place in her heart.

"Chol Makyn, my dear boy," she said, beginning her ancient ritual, making elaborate hand motions over my body. Stiffening from head to toe, I felt squeezed, as if one of her many snakes had finally caught me. She called to *Atim* to have favor on me.

My heart pounded and I was ashamed. I cast my eyes to the floor and could not look at her. Awkwardly, I moved away from her and sat on one of her mats with my head down. I was torn between honoring my grandmother and rejecting her cultish practices. She did not miss the snub, and her face blanched. She turned her back toward me and resumed preparing the evening meal. The tension between us was heavy, and I was grateful when Joseph came in along with other mothers and fathers.

We all assembled in the eating area. I looked around to see if any of grandmother's large, black snakes were near. I never knew where I might find one, coiled in the corner or under a basket. To kill the snakes was prohibited. They were thought to be sacred to *Atim*. They must be invited into one's home and treated with honor. Our meal began the way it always did in Grandfather's house. Grandfather took a little milk from the table, which he kept in a hollow gourd, and walked reverently to the family shrine, a black and gray mass of snake skins, animal teeth, and bones, littered with offerings. He poured a small amount of milk on it to honor and pacify Atim.

"I hope he will be pleased with our offering," said Grandfather as he walked casually back to his seat. We all fell silent, troubled by what was happening. My grandparents were unaware of our feelings. They were merely doing what our people had done for centuries. We looked to Elijah for guidance. He appeared deep in thought, troubled, with his eyes closed and head bent. Joseph poked me in the leg and gave me a knowing look. I wanted to get up and run from the table. It is always troubling to be a child when the adults are in conflict. After a moment, Elijah cleared his throat to speak.

"Grandfather," said Elijah. "We want to honor you, but we can no longer honor your customs. We no longer give our reverence to the gods of our ancestors. We have one God and one great ancestor, Jesus Christ. We have all been registered up."

"Registered up" was how our village came to describe new Christians since they were no longer completely of this world, but "going up." Grandfather and Grandmother looked at Elijah in bewilderment. They didn't understand this change and were hurt and confused.

"You cannot say these horrible things, Elijah, or you will surely die" Grandfather said, pleading with him. He was terribly concerned, afraid for Elijah. Grandmother was silent and then she said, "Elijah, Atim will not take this lightly." Her face was drawn in tight lines.

"I have no fear of Atim," said Elijah. He threw his hands up in a gesture of abandon and then pointed to the heavens. "Jesus is more powerful than all our gods!"

Grandfather was taken aback, shocked by these words. Grandmother slapped her hand on the ground in anger. Elijah did not budge, and I could feel a dividing line being drawn between the two generations of my family. We were still one tribe, one clan, and one family, but something had changed. The ancient fabric was indeed unraveling. That evening as we were leaving, Grandmother again began her ritual over me. Elijah looked stricken and took hold of me protectively, laying his large arm over my shoulder.

"Grandmother," he said. "I am sorry, but you must stop these things. He is special to God and registered up now."

Grandmother stopped what she was doing, confused, and then resignation came over her face. I so longed for her to understand that it wasn't personal. We weren't rejecting her, but we felt compelled to reject the old spiritual order. Before we left, I heard mother speaking to her in a quiet, soothing voice.

"Mother we are thankful to our ancestors and we will always honor you, but we have a new God now." I couldn't hear what Grandmother said, but I knew they embraced and I hoped that we could have peace within our family.

I went home that night troubled. As I lay on my mat, I could see the moonlight shining through the cracks in the walls. Joseph was breathing lightly, and I could hear the quiet murmur of Mother and Father whispering to each other in the night. I closed my eyes and focused on God and I felt him with me, just as Elijah had promised. I knew that, because of Jesus, I would always have a family in Christ, even as my earthly family experienced trouble and change. This lesson would prove itself through the years with the tragedies that lay waiting for my family, because the fabric of our shared life would not simply be pulled apart, but destroyed. We didn't know then, that in the middle of our own spiritual battles, there was another battle, and it was being waged throughout the villages of Southern Sudan like a violent circle closing in on us. It was a battle for money, power, religion, and identity. It was not simply a battle, but a civil war with lost flesh and blood, and it was coming for us.

Chapter Six

THE ONE THING WE HAD

Weeks of running through bullets, debris, and ashes had changed us. We were a different set of boys, most of whom I didn't recognize. I wondered if I would even recognize myself. I had no mirror, but I was sure if I saw myself, a different John would look back at me. My eyes were sharper, my body lean, and my thoughts were mostly of water and food. After the Civil War became full blown and my village was invaded. I was forced to run for my life for months. When I finally arrived at the refugee camp, it was a melee of volunteers shouting in English, boys crying, and the speaking of different languages, ones I had never heard before. I collapsed on the dry land with only the trees to cover me. Many of the boys around me sat down to rest and died there from starvation or untreated wounds. I can remember someone raising my head to drink water. I could feel its coolness on my cracked lips, running down my parched throat. "Where are we?" I asked the faceless person, as if waking from a dream. His face was eclipsed by the sun, and my hunger was so gnawing that I was dizzy.

"You're in Ethiopia," the stranger said, giving me one last drink and walking away to attend the others. Ethiopia was a faraway place I had only heard of once or twice. Since the days of my infancy, I had never left my small village, and here I was alone, stranded in a foreign country. I looked into the distance and it was formless with dirt stretching on for miles. Only our bodies and a few trees filled this empty place. I prayed silently that God would help me stay alive and go home someday. He healed Aluong, I thought. Couldn't he help me now?

That strange place was called the Dimma Refugee Camp. It was new, a sprawling strip of unsettled land with nothing in it. We young refugees were commanded to stay there and make do, but with what? That was the question on all our minds. There was nothing but land, and the terrain was so alien from what we shepherd boys were used to. It seemed that everything we had learned on how to survive served no purpose in this desolate world. We didn't know how long we would be here in this place that did not belong to us. I was afraid that we would die here all alone.

It was a winter night in Ethiopia. A little boy in my group lay next to me shivering. The night time was always the worst. I draped a blanket over him, hoping to keep him warm through the night. Being from South Sudan, we had never experienced cold, and here we felt a piercing chill in the air. Boys had died from pneumonia, and the small *tukul* we built out of fallen branches and a flimsy tarp could never hold out against the Ethiopian wind. It rushed through our tent and blew against our mostly bare bodies. At that time, few of us owned clothes. Some of us had been given blankets and shorts by the UN which made the conditions more bearable.

As I lay still in the night, the shivering of the boy slowly lessened and his breathing became rhythmic. My mind wandered to tomorrow's work. Recently, we had divided into groups and I was chosen as the leader, a great responsibility. The days were constant and steady work. Tomorrow it was my turn to wait in the food lines. I would be there all day. We had developed a roster for who would have to wait in line to receive the red beans the UN gave us. We had wheat flour, sugar, oil, and beans. Some of the other boys were scheduled to cook, but of course none of us knew how. We made plain, course food. The night wind rasped loudly against the fragile tarp and the structure swayed in the wind. I felt a new weariness creep over me as I made a mental list of what we needed to do. My heart was not yet broken. There was no time for heartbreak. I had to survive. I thought back to Mother, Father, Joseph, Aluong, and Elijah, but I couldn't let my mind rest on those thoughts. We were still fighting for our lives.

I began the day by gathering the boys together. An older boy and I walked around our *Tukul* calling to the younger boys in the camp to come join us. They had been playing and talking, calling to one another in the morning sun. The little boys came and plopped down on the dusty ground.

"Let's see your feet," I said. The older boy and I went around and look at each foot carefully. We discovered that this was something that had to be done daily, because boys, especially the little, helpless ones, were dying of *tut tut*. Small bugs burrowed their way into their feet, digging under the nail bed. Sometimes they lost their toes, but sometimes worst. The disease could spread to the joints of the entire body. The feet would swell, ending the ability to walk. It was not unusual to see little boys hobbling on swollen feet.

"You must check your feet every day," the older boy scolded the little ones, the frustration evident in his voice. He was getting tired. We all were getting tired. We had been eating better. Food trucks were coming daily, and we were able to wait in the food lines to receive our portions, but disease was everywhere. We had no clean source of water. We all drank and washed in the over-crowded river. There were no latrines, so people had to relieve themselves nearby. The camp had grown so fast in the past five months that there was no working clinic. We had already lost boys from diarrhea, measles, malaria, cholera, and pneumonia.

Gunshot wounds festered, and diseases, left untreated, developed and spread.

"Every older boy," I said to group, calling them to attention "pick a younger one to look after. You must go to the river and clean his feet every day. I don't want to lose anyone to *tut tut*."

The five and seven year olds lined up with the teenagers. I prayed to God that we wouldn't lose any more boys and that the *tut tut* wouldn't get us. The younger ones looked so weak and vulnerable. They need their mamas, I thought.

Before we disbanded, I counted the boys. There were thirty. This meant one was missing. I would have to find him. My heart pounded. I counted once more. There were definitely thirty. Maybe he has gone off searching for food. When a boy went missing, I never knew if he had wandered off, perhaps found a different group, or if he would turn up dead. One boy had been missing for so long that it took me six months to find him. The camp was so large and congested. He had gotten lost and banded together with another group.

"We have lost a boy," I told them. "Keep an eye out for him." I turned and headed toward the food lines. As I walked, I stopped at *tukul* after *tukul* asking after him. No one had seen him. He has most likely found a relative, I thought. That would be so good. Maybe he is reunited with his cousin, as one of the other boys had been months earlier. After hours in the lines, I returned with red beans to cook for our daily meal. We only received food for one meal a day, and we had quickly discovered it was always better to eat at night and be hungry during the day because it was hard to sleep on an empty belly. Then I saw the boy who had been lost, sitting outside our *tukul*, leaning listlessly on one of the heavy branches we used for benches. With his head resting in his hands, he was slumped over in an unnatural way.

"What's wrong little one?" I asked, as I approached him. He was only six years old, the same age as Joseph the last time I saw him. I was approaching fourteen. He looked at me. His nose was crusted with snot and his eyes swollen from tears. He was always crying. I would hear him crying at night, during the day, always. He was inconsolable, his face slick with tears. He never wanted to play soccer with other boys. He didn't look for food or care to eat. I had seen boys like this before. They died of a grieving heart. They just gave up. He turned to me. His eyes were glazed and yellow and I knew that he was in danger.

"God is with you," I told him, resting my hand on his shoulder. I could feel how fragile he was, the bones sticking through his flesh. "I know you are sad, but God will save us," I promised him. His eyes filled with tears and I knew he wanted his family. He wanted to go home to his mother and father, to the cattle and the rich fields. He wanted to be a shepherd boy again. We all did.

"We are making beans. Why don't you go and help," I said. He looked away, watching the boys play soccer, but not quite seeing anything. Later that night we tried to force him to eat some of the beans and drink water. He took one bite and lay down to sleep. He never woke up. The next morning we found his cold body on the ground. I wished I knew his full name. That always troubled me when we lost someone. How could we tell his family? They needed to know.

We gathered silently beside him. Many of the boys started to cry. We remembered how at night when we gathered together around the fire to cook our evening meal, he would talk of his family. He would tell us about his parents, his sisters and brothers, those whom he danced with, the songs and the stories by his family hearth, and the vigorous, communal life of the cattle camps. We knew he died of a broken heart. This was the true cause of his death. He had lost hope and surrendered. His body had simply followed his dying spirit. I looked at the boys, the sadness and fear in their resigned faces. They wondered if this could happen to them. They knew what we had to do next. I could feel heaviness in our souls. The older boys and I lifted him off the ground and began to carry him. We formed a small procession; the older boys carried his body at the front of the line, and the little boys walked in the back. We could hear them crying quietly behind us. We took him as far away from the camp as we could and brought him to a place near the river that was shaded by a few trees. We worked together to dig a shallow grave. We didn't have a shovel, so we used our hands and a few sticks. Placing him in the ground, the boys listened as I offered a humble prayer, though I knew of no prayer to fit the moment.

"Jesus, this little boy has died. He died, Jesus, because of sin. He was too sad to go on. I know that in you there is life and there is family. Please give these things to him now and bless him." His little body lay crumpled in the ground, as we slowly began to cover him with dirt.

"What would his mother think?" I thought. She needed to be here. It was wrong to bury him without his parents, his brothers, sisters, and uncles. We knew instinctively that we were too young to be performing such a rite. It had a gravity and solemnity that was too much for our young souls.

In my group we had buried five boys and he would be the sixth. I never forgot these burials. They stayed with me over the years. I remembered each boy we laid in the ground, and my heart cried out in a wordless prayer. I couldn't even speak or think, but I was praying, crying out to God somewhere deep inside me. I wanted God to do something. The way I knew he could. He had healed Aluong, couldn't he help us now?

In time, things in the camp got a little better. We were rationed one daily meal, and we no longer had to skip days of eating. We were beginning to play soccer for longer periods during the day, and we would come together at night and cook our food. We banded together as a community. The UN was able to set up a working clinic to take care of the sick. They began to offer a few classes under the trees. I loved this. It had been so long since I had learned anything. I liked to sit under the trees and think about things other than the sad things I saw. I learned English and finished my first class with ease. I looked forward to learning more of the language. It helped me communicate with several Ethiopians and UN people. I turned fifteen and became a Standard One pupil, the U.S. equivalent of the first grade.

One day after school, we all sat down together. The sun was beginning to fade and our *tukul* provided some shade from the heat. We passed around our red beans. I was hungry from not having eaten all day. The boys tore into their food. I bowed my head and said, "Thank you, Jesus. Amen." The boys often looked at me curiously when I prayed. We were from different parts of Sudan and many of them, like my own family and people, had never heard of Elijah's God. "Why do you say those words?" asked one boy. "You are always saying something strange and we don't understand you."

"I don't know," I said. I tried to collect my thoughts, but it had been so long since I had talked of these things. "In my village my uncle, Aluong, was so sick that he nearly died. The *jak* never cured him. There was only one *jok* who did, the *jok* of Jesus Christ." I still had select Scriptures memorized, and I recited them to myself. I was still so young, and although I had seen the power of the gospel, I knew little of what the Bible actually said or what other Christians thought. I had never even owned a Bible, except for the times Elijah had let me carry his. I knew only of the miraculous things I had seen in my village and the teaching Elijah had given me as a boy. I didn't know what it was to follow

Jesus outside of Baping, or what his other followers were like. I could, however, never forget the things Elijah had told me, that Christ overcame suffering, that there was life in him, and that he gave you a new identity and family. Such knowledge was precious to me. I had mentally stored it up over the years and would often bring these truths to mind like presents being opened. They gave me strength. Johnson's prophecy that I would no longer cry but proclaim God's Word, was still somewhere hidden in my thoughts, silently encouraging me on.

"Why was the *Jok* of Jesus Christ able to save your uncle?" the boy asked, looking at me intently as he finished with his beans. All the boys were now listening to our conversation and I could tell they had wondered about these things for some time but were only asking now. I found thirty or so earnest faces staring at me.

"Jesus is the only true *Jok*." I paused, hesitating for a moment, trying to grasp the right words to describe the mystery and then they came to me. Elijah's teaching was on my lips. It was as if some great hand came and rested on my shoulder and a voice whispered the words in my ear. I continued on. "Actually, he is more than the *jok,* much more," I found I was excited to share these truths. How long had it been since I had talked at length about the God of Heaven. "He is God. He is Nhialic made known. He can do things that the other *jak* can't. He is most powerful, but he is also our friend. He looks after us. He gives us a family. He overcomes death. In fact, once he died, but he was raised from the dead."

Surprise washed over their faces. I looked down at the dry, barren ground and thought of our young friend who was now covered with it. "He overcomes death," I said once more, almost as if I were hearing the words anew, and I realized they meant more to me now than ever before.

"And this Jesus is your friend?" a boy asked.

"Oh yes," I nodded. A memory flickered in my mind of a warm summer evening in Baping as we crowded together in our neighbor's *tukul*. Elijah peered over his Bible, sweat on his brow, teaching us truth as the Spirit of God filled our hearts.

"He was raised from the dead and he raises all his people from the dead. When you follow Jesus, you're promised eternal life."

Those last words had impact. I watched as they slowly sunk in. I could see their incredulity, the joyful mystery etched on their faces. We had lost so much. I knew they must be thinking of their families.

"He takes away our sins, so we no longer have to sacrifice bulls and chickens," I said. The ideas were now coming to my mind with great momentum. I felt compelled to share. They were all deep in thought, weighing the truth of my words, even the little ones.

"What is sin?" a young boy asked.

I remembered a conversation that took place with Elijah so long ago and how I had asked the same question. I went to cattle camps in search of sin until I finally understood what he meant. "I have seen sin," I told him proudly. His words now came to me, "You will see even more than this."

"Look around you," I said. "Sin is everywhere. You don't have to look far. The first time I saw sin was a boy beating his little brother with a stick as if he were a cow. It was a sin. A sin is when they came to kill us in our villages. It's a sin when we hurt each other and say cruel things."

These were the sins we committed, the sins of our hearts, and the sins committed against us. These were not hard to see. It was because of sin that we had to bury our own. It was because of sin that our mothers and fathers were gone. It was because of sin we were forced to live in a place that was no place at all. And death, death was everywhere.

The other boys in the group saw what I saw as well. When they heard the precious things I knew, that Jesus could save them from sin and death, they responded with intense interest. It began a never-ending conversation. They wanted to know everything I knew about God. As we walked to the river or gathered wood for the fire, they asked questions.

"Can your *jok* really save us from death?" one asked.

"Yes, he can." I said. "I have seen it. He saved my uncle from death."

"How does God give you a new family?" asked another.

"Everyone who follows Jesus is his sister or brother. That means we are all sisters and brothers. He is our great ancestor."

At night, when I prayed for my food, they joined me and we slowly began to pray together. Something in my heart began to lift. My thoughts were no longer burdened by food, water, and shelter. There was something more to life. Something, rather someone, was with us. It was Jesus who was hopeful and true, and we could all share in him as brothers.

The new truth we were experiencing was not only in my group, it was also spreading throughout the camp. I began to see and hear more and more people praying. We began meeting for worship under the trees on Sunday. Most of the men from our villages had been killed, so there were many widows in the camp. They started to come regularly to check on us and invite us to worship. I remember four women who led the prayers and organized the services. They became our pastors. I was happy to see so many others who knew about Jesus. We frequently met to sing songs and pray. The talk around the camp changed. People were asking about Jesus--who he was, what was he like and how could he rescue?

There was an Anglican priest who came to the camp and offered some basic Bible instruction. After that, it seemed that

Jesus was everywhere and in everything. We all wanted to know him or know more about him. A Catholic priest came and baptized several hundred people. An Anglican priest came, and he baptized thousands of people, baptizing people all day long for nearly a week.

With the newly baptized, everything changed. A new current was pulsing through the camp. The worship services grew in number. We woke up early in the morning and prayed and sang songs until it became too hot. After the sun went down, we met again and stayed late into the evening. There were hundreds of baptisms every Sunday. The talk around the camp was high-spirited, "Oh, are you baptized? Have you gotten a new name? What is your name? Have your learned this new song?"

Christian names became meaningful because they were so new. They represented new life and freedom. For refugees who had lost everything, a new identity was a gift. We began to see that we were not displaced unknowns, but God's people. We were refugees in God. We sensed that what had been lost to us, our dignity, had been returned. We received a new status -one as real persons.

Sitting under the trees with my fellow refugees, I felt the worship transform our hearts, souls, and minds. I longed for my drum. There were many different preachers in camp. Some of them were new pastors, others were visiting, and some were even new Christians, but these sermons reached us. God was speaking to us. "You are a new person. You have a new identity. You have a new community. You are given new life in Christ. Don't worry if you don't have parents. God is your parent. You have lost your people. You now belong to God's people." These were the messages that were preached. This news overcame our despair.

We were given some Bibles and we took turns reading. We often met for informal Bible studies where we heard the powerful words the book contained. "Jesus says, 'Love one another,'" the leader of the study told us. "This means we take care of each other. Don't worry because there is another life after this one. This is not all there is."

We didn't know where we were headed or what would happen next. We didn't know if we would see our loved ones again. We had nothing of our own, except a blanket and a pair of shorts. We didn't have resources, connections, or any way of advancement. We were orphaned and lost without family. But with this truth, a steady hope arose. It was the one and only true thing we had. The one thing we could cling too. Our worship was our dignity, our comfort, and our family. I felt the truth of it grow in my heart. It had been there all along, but life had tried to choke it out of me, but the truth won. After all, Jesus had healed Aluong hadn't he? So, of course, it must all be true.

Chapter Seven
CROSSING

They came with guns and soldiers on foot. They came with their uniforms, vehicles, and arsenals. We had no warning, no plan of action, and no means of defense. We were mostly children, some women, and a few elderly. Sick and hungry, weak from years of refugee life, we weren't prepared to fight. Why did they attack us? We were no threat to them. Why not just ask us to leave? It made no sense, and yet, they came. Once again, we had a decision, die or run. So we ran, but first we had to cross the River Rhad. How many more of us would we lose?

Days before this inevitable crossing, I found myself in the mid-afternoon heat, standing in the food lines at Dimma, waiting for our daily ration. Yesterday's food had not come, and we went without. Today, I would stand in this line for hours, as long as it took. The other boys were counting on me to bring provisions. I had been standing for so long that I had forgotten when I arrived. I thought a few hours had passed. They had run out of food, and we were waiting for more food trucks to arrive. Hunger kept me going, forcing me to ignore the daze I was in. The woman in front of me was weak and tired and sat on the ground. The wind blew at my back, making little kernels of dirt pelt my skin. The barren land of Ethiopia stretched out before us, flat and dusty. In recent weeks our food rations had dwindled, and we had all grown so thin. We were losing energy and our hope was being shaken. As

I squinted in the heat, I swore it looked like some of my fellow refuges might blow away in the wind. They were like paper. The wind in Dimma was fierce, with a life of its own.

Years had gone by in Dimma, and we had banded together as a family, but we were still strangers in this land. God had met us in this place, but I often wondered if we would ever have the chance to leave it. How long would we be stuck here? I remembered our life in the village and how we lived in comfort with the world around us. I missed the cows and our way of life. At the time, I couldn't wait to get out of the cattle camps, but now, I missed being a shepherd boy. Here there were only wild beasts that snatched children in the night.

As I waited, I prayed and collected my nervous thoughts. Lately, I had felt that there was some change occurring in the camp, but no one knew the details. Information is scarce in a refugee camp. It wasn't just that our food rations were slimming, but we noticed that the volunteers were slowly leaving. A few weeks earlier, we stopped having school. It was unsettling. There was talk of political unrest or even war in Ethiopia. We didn't know what to believe. We were so isolated, without newspapers or television, and our news came only by word of mouth. I saw food trucks rolling by and felt a surge of relief. It would be soon now.

When I returned with food for our group, we quickly fell in line and began our tasks: starting the fire, cooking rice, and sharing the water between ourselves. We were hungry and there was no time to waste before nightfall. The fire grew hot as the sun settled in the sky and the cool night air came in. Whether we had food or not, we always spent the evenings around the fire, but that night we were blessed. God had provided for us. We could barely fit in our *tukul*, so we lived mostly outdoors, running through the camp, visiting other boys, and playing games. We had created benches out of fallen wood, and there we met for our Bible studies and theological discussions.

We gathered round the fire. "Let us pray," I said to the boys. We all bowed our heads and I said a short prayer, thanking Jesus for our food. That night we were silent as we fell upon our food. We were all so hungry. The feet of the little boy next to me were swollen with *jigger*, we still couldn't escape that disease. I looked around the circle and noticed how much we had changed. We had lost boys. Some we buried, some drifted to different camps, and others went looking for family members. Thirty boys had become fifteen and we varied in ages six to sixteen. It was a mystery how we came together, running through the bush, seeking shelter, and then the UN came, dividing us and making us into official units. We had been a family these past years, a family of orphans, but still a family. We didn't know that we had been given the name "Lost Boys of Sudan."

"I ran into someone I knew today," said a boy in my group, a little older than myself, maybe fifteen years of age. He was a leader in our group and helped us make important decisions. We waited to hear if this was a positive meeting or not. Meetings with acquaintances could often bring terrible news, especially of lost loved ones.

"He told me that there is war in Ethiopia and that rebels came to the Pinyadoo camp and killed refugees."

No one spoke as the fear spread among us. Something about this rang true to me. It would explain all the changes in the camp, but I couldn't understand why rebels would kill Sudanese refugees. We were no threat to them. We were without guns or money. We were defenseless. Most of us weren't even fighting age. This couldn't be, I told myself. It was irrational.

"Why would they attack Sudanese?" I asked.

"When we were in our homeland, before the invasions, my cousin was a member of the Sudanese People's Liberation Army.

Many of them were trained by communist Ethiopian soldiers. He said that these new Ethiopian rebel groups link us with the old communist government. They think we all might be part of the SPLA. They want no part of the old communist regime."

He looked into the camp fire. The lines on his face hardened and glistened in the fire light. Something was wrong. I could feel it; we all could. We had sensed it for weeks. The night was now black, and the food was not sticking to our stomachs. We were tired.

"Maybe we should try and leave," the little boy with the wounded feet suggested.

This had occurred to me. If we left we would be without food or shelter, but then again, these things were hardly guaranteed in Dimma. Could the little boys, the weaker boys, withstand another trek? How could they make it? But the real question was, where could we go? Ethiopia wasn't safe. We were stranded here.

"We could go back to Sudan, to our homeland," the little one suggested.

He looked up at me from his position by the fire, and I could see the desire to return in his young eyes. The idea stirred something in me as well. Some hope I had long buried. I knew they felt it too, but it was impossible. I wished I could tell him we were going home, back to our villages, back to our mothers and fathers, back to shepherding, back to life along the Nile. What a joy it would be to see his is mother embracing him after years of separation. Washing his feet, she would nurse him back to health, and all would be well again.

"Our homeland has been destroyed," said a young man, a fellow leader. He was becoming angry, angry at us, angry at the situation. "It has been overtaken by the North. If we return, we will all be killed."

I looked at my group. We had all been through so much and some of them, like the little boy next to me with his wounded feet, were young and vulnerable. He couldn't run again. We were trapped.

"Sudan is the only place we can go," said another boy. He began to draw a map on the ground with his finger, showing us the options.

We discussed at length the direction we could take. My mind raced with ideas. I thought back to certain volunteers who had taken an interest in me. Maybe I could find a way to contact them. I wasn't sure how I could do that. I had no way of communicating, but there had to be some way out of this situation.

We waited, thought, and talked late into the evening until exhaustion overtook us. I settled down on the hard floor. I had given away my blanket long ago. I knew I wouldn't sleep. I could hear the soft breathing of the other boys, and the moon shone through our *tukul*. I listened to the familiar sound of the tarp trembling in the wind. It was a moment of peace, to lie on the ground, not having to fight or scavenge for food, but I was troubled. If we returned to Sudan, we had no idea what would face us there, most likely a hostile new government. I remembered the day when they invaded and how we had been hunted through the forest. But, would Dimma continue to be safe? We never knew if what we heard was true or simply rumor. How I wished Elijah was here to help guide me, but I knew what he would say. That there was another guide I could turn to even greater than himself. I prayed in a whisper, "Jesus help us." I closed my eyes and remembered how Paul looked the day he was healed. How he rubbed his nose in disbelief. I could never forget the joy, the gratitude, the overflow of goodness we experienced. "I know you are here," I said to Jesus. "I know you are good." That night I resolved to try and contact a volunteer I knew, perhaps a pastor. Maybe I could send a letter or visit another camp. There had to be some way out of this.

In the morning, I noticed that the food trucks hadn't arrived. It had been a day without food, and we were getting worried. I decided to try and find a volunteer. Some of the boys were playing soccer. Others were sitting, talking in the sun. Some were laid out with *jigger* or *tut tut*. There were a few women and older people flocked together in little groups. I made my way through the maze and activity of camp life, at times stopping to chat briefly, but I was determined to try and reach someone I knew who had some answers. I saw a young boy from my group frantically waving at me. He was trying to tell me something. I started in his direction and then stopped.

Everything went still for one spilt second, and then I heard it. There was a scream and then the sound of machine guns. Dust filled the air and a young boy collapsed not far from me, blood pouring from him, his body shuddering.

"No, no, no, no," I thought.

With my mind ringing and my heart thundering inside me, and I was off running, running as fast as I could. I could hear them behind me, more gunshots and more screams. As I ran, I saw a big artillery vehicle with soldiers, boys not much older than myself, perhaps seventeen to twenty years of age. They were shouting at us, commanding us to run, to leave their country or die. "Who are they? Why are they here? Rebels," I thought. "It had to be the rebels." I just kept running. I could see my *tukul* in the distance. I was screaming at the boys and waving my arms, "Run! Get out! Get out!" Where were they? I couldn't see them. They must have taken off running as well. We were all lost in the confusion and terror. I ran, my body beginning to spasm. I looked for the little one with *jigger*. I wanted to carry him, to take him with me. I didn't see him anywhere. We were yelling to each other as we ran. "Make it to the river," we called to each other, "Make it the river!"

I ran and ran with the gunshots behind me and the river somewhere ahead of me, ominous and wild. Finally, we reached the banks of the river. We collapsed to catch our breath, heaving on the river bank. I was shivering all over. I tried to talk to someone, but my teeth were chattering. Somebody grabbed me by the arm and pulled me toward the river's edge. He was a stronger boy, older than I was. I didn't even see his face, only the river looming ahead of us.

"We have to cross this river," he shouted.

I looked out at the long stretch of gray water. Boys had died in this river. They had drowned or been eaten by crocodiles. The river had swallowed them up. It was the rainy season and the river was all but overflowing. I wanted to throw up, but I was rigid, so tense with fear.

"Join hands," the boy shouted. "We will form a chain."

He stepped into the water, his knees slowly disappearing into the deep. I grabbed hold of the boy in front of me, gripping his hand as fiercely as he gripped mine, and I extended my other hand to the boy behind me, and we formed a chain. I felt the water, cold creeping upward toward my knees. The ringing in my head cleared. My heart thudded against my chest and I tried to breathe. I turned to look one last time. Boys were still running toward the water's edge. Some were wounded, bleeding. They were joining hands as well, preparing themselves to cross. In the distance I could hear the screams and weeping, the guns, and artillery.

The leader of the chain was covered in water now. His head bobbed just above the surface of the water. He called to us one last time over his shoulder, and I knew he was about to lose his footing. The river was getting deeper and deeper. We would all soon be surrendered to its current.

"Whatever happens," he shouted, his voice ringing out to us across the waves, "do not let go of each other."

Chapter Eight
RUNNING THROUGH THORNS

The earth was caked to our feet, feet hardened from years of running. I reached down to pull out the thorns from my feet and legs. The others in my group took a moment to sit and rest. They were breathing heavily and groaning in pain. We had been running in the bush for days, if not weeks by now. The boy next to me had a gunshot wound that was bleeding through the shirt which had been wrapped tightly around it. It was surely festering by now. Others were in even worse shape. Many more had been left behind, swallowed up by the river, food for the crocodiles. Our numbers had dwindled and we looked bad. I knew that if we did not find shelter, food, and water soon, we would all be dead. The sun was beating down on us and sweat poured down my back. I looked around the bush, searching the area for water and saw nothing. Don't think about the thirst, I told myself.

We found that we were, once again, trapped in a place that seemed like nowhere. We could not go back to Ethiopia to face the hostile rebels, but we couldn't remain in Sudan. We had been in our homeland for a few short weeks and had already been attacked. When we crossed the Rhad, we thought we had reached safety, but the government was there. The NIF heard that we had been forced to flee Ethiopia and were returning to Sudan. They sent their armies. They came, began air raids, and fired shots from the sky. They captured the town of Pochala, attacking both refugees and civilians. We were now heading in the only direction we could, to the Kenyan border.

I looked at my feet and grimaced in pain. How I wanted to lie down and rest for the day. I closed my eyes and imagined I was back in my village, sitting in the doorway of my *tukul,* drinking cool, fresh milk from a hollow gourd. I shrugged off the thought and tried to ignore my bloated, thirsty tongue. I pulled myself up to get going again, and we all fell in line walking together. Hopefully, we would find water soon. I was still with my group, although we had lost members since Dimma. We were a new group of boys, all mixed together. That was how we lived, banding together when we could, only to find ourselves separated again. We formed and reformed our communities in the bush many times. The afternoon sun continued to burn down on us, creating a dizzying effect. I could feel my footsteps growing unsteady, but I kept moving. We had to be close to the border. We had heard that there were volunteers in Kenya, rescuing people, providing food and drink. If only we could get to that point without dying of thirst or being attacked by the military men. We knew they were still behind us.

We saw an elderly man lying still in the bush, with branches covering him, shielding him from the sun. I thought he was dead, but he called out to us.

"Help me," he said, his voice weak and strained. He had been left to die. "I don't want to die here." His was talking clearly and was in relatively good condition except for his feet which were a bloody, swollen mess.

"I can no longer walk," he said. He looked up at us, pleading, desperate for help. I looked at the boys in my group. It was clear we had reached an agreement. I could tell by their faces that we would help him. Ours was a culture that held great respect for the elderly. We had been instructed to care for them our whole lives. We had no choice, but I knew what it meant for us. We were barely hanging on ourselves.

"Let's see if we can carry him," I said. We gathered around, picking him up by his arms and legs. Tears of relief came to his eyes. He was still alive and wanted to go on, but he was so helpless. The man was heavy, and I didn't know how we could do it, but we knew we needed to try. We would take turns carrying him. There were many trekking through the forest with thorns and bullets in their bodies. There were several others, like this man, whose feet were so badly wounded from running through thorns that they could no longer walk.

We carried the man for several days. We had no food and very little water. I focused my mind on getting to the Kenyan border. It was always just a couple of steps ahead. I pictured it with every footstep. I was getting closer and closer. I watched the bodies of my friends being transformed before my eyes. They were so dehydrated, their skin was once again like shattered glass. "We are drying up," I thought. I noticed how many of the boys' bodies began to crack open, spilling blood. Hours later they collapsed and died, simply falling on the ground. There was no time to bury them; we had to keep moving or we would be next.

My friend and I began to stumble under the weight of the man. He looked at me and I knew what he was thinking. The pain and exhaustion was too much. We all tumbled to the ground. The old man began to cry. Struggling to stand, one of the boys wordlessly pushed me forward, leaving the man behind us. I looked back at the old man one last time. I stared at him helplessly, and in that moment, I wanted to collapse on the ground beside him. My friend pushed me forward again.

"Go on," he cried, pushing me again, "Go, now."

He was crying as he pushed me along. We both were. Our sweat and tears mixed together, but we kept going. We could hear the man's frantic screams behind us, calling to us, begging us to help him.

"Maybe some others will rescue him," I thought. It was the only way I could bring myself to leave him, but I knew he would die or be shot by the military men who were pursuing us. Hot tears poured down my cheeks as the sound of his cries grew fainter. I looked down on the ground in front of me, attempting to focus only on my steps, one foot in front of the other. As we stumbled along I began to wonder. "Why must this go on? How long, Jesus, could we continue running?"

More days passed. No food and so little water. I saw boys attempt to drink their own urine. It didn't work. I was sure that we would die, that this last and final trek had killed us.

We heard the sounds of the border before we reached it, the sound of buses and the sound of volunteers calling out commands. We saw the other refugees huddled together. We were met by the Kenyan government and the UN. I fell to my knees, unable to carry on. I could no longer keep my eyes open. I had the sensation that if I stayed there even a little longer, I would dry up and turn to dust. There were several large vehicles prepared to take us someplace. "Where," I wondered, "where else could we possibly go?"

Chapter Nine
KAKUMA

I came back to my group with a surprise, a small brown bag in my hands. The boys eyed it curiously and gathered around. The UN had been handing out brown bags of food to refugees all day. It was the most food I had seen since Baping. I slowly began to unload its contents, one by one.

"We have sugar, salt, oil, wheat flour, rice, and red beans," I said showing each item to the group as if it were a coveted prize. We were beaming in tandem. "And that is not all. We can go to the food lines twice a day. That means two meals a day." We cheered and laughed. That was the most food we had received in a very long time. It had been four years since I had eaten more than one meal a day.

As we gathered the wood for our fire, we laughed and talked. The Kakuma refugee camp along the Kenyan border had proved better than I had expected. Not only were we given more food, but also pots, pans, a few utensils, and clothes. I was chosen to be group leader again, but all these boys were in early adolescence if not full teenagers. There were no little ones to worry about. They had either died along the journey or were now grown. We could all take care of ourselves. Kakuma was the official refugee camp for the South Sudanese, the vast majority of us were lost boys, but there were women, elderly men, and even a few entire families. These families were very blessed to have stayed together.

When we left Dimma, I thought we were close to forty thousand. Now we appeared to be only seventeen thousand. Crocodiles, bombs, and thorns had killed so many. Thankfully, the Kenyan government allowed us to settle along the border. It was a desert place, windy and hot, quite different from the climate of Ethiopia with its large green trees. We gathered around the fire and ate our food. We made *ugali*, a kind of grits covered with sugar. I licked my lips and swore I had never tasted anything so delicious.

The under-tree school was rustic, established by the UN and Kenyan government. I found my place in the large group of students. The UN volunteer was a young, American woman. She held a globe of the world and showed us the different countries. She talked in English, and I surprised myself with how much I understood. I never missed a day when school was in session, which was off and on due to the instability of our situation. I wished I could spend the whole day at school, but I knew that in a few short hours I would need to return to my group. There were some students, a select few, who were sent to the UN school. They were the very brightest, perhaps one or two out of three hundred ever qualified. Even on my best days, I scored in the middle, never at the top.

Elijah had always encouraged me to learn. I remember how I used to sit near Uncle and listen to him tell stories from the Bible. After finishing his story, he asked probing questions to see how much I retained. I was expected to learn and memorize these lessons, and it mattered when I prayed for the people or recited the Scriptures in church. No one expected much from me in the camp. The regularity of the school was tenuous. Given the availability of volunteers and the political climate, there were often long breaks, and classes always ended by twelve when the heat grew unbearable. For the remainder of the day we could do as we pleased, and the boys and I played soccer for long hours.

That night by the fire side, eating my second meal, I thanked God for how far I had come. I had lived through so many challenges. I wondered if there was a purpose behind them. Here I was alive and eating two meals a day. I knew I should be thankful, but my heart was restless.

I wanted to learn more, to do something with my life, but my opportunities were so limited. If I lived in Baping, perhaps, I would have become like Elijah, a spiritual leader to my people, or become a shepherd like my father. It was hard to see a future here.

It wasn't simply that we had no future, but we had not established a sense of community or identity as we had at Dimma. We were a society that had come together due to violence and war, emerging out of shared trauma. The groups themselves were groups in form only. No one was accountable to anyone else in any real or lasting way. We were mostly young boys and teenagers. We could leave our groups when we pleased. We had no family system of responsibility or mutual giving, receiving, and sharing. There was no one to guide us or take care of us who would remain committed to us over the critical years of childhood and young adulthood. There was love and friendship among us, but our groups existed for logistical purposes only.

Later that evening, long after we had fallen asleep, a small band of boys snuck back into our *tukul*. They were talking loudly, swaggering, stepping on us, and bragging of how they spent the night talking to girls at a night club. I had never tasted alcohol, but I knew instantly what the sour smell was. This was happening more and more. Boys were joining gangs. They were traveling into the nearby cities, making small things, and peddling on the streets for money, spending their earnings in night clubs. They bragged to us of their exploits, how much they drank, and how many girls they talked to. We were boys becoming men, and we had no clear path or future ahead of us. These boys, languishing in futility, were turning to whatever made them feel better or important. We were all searching. I closed my eyes trying to block out the sound and fall back to sleep, but my mind was too awake. It wasn't the first night I was kept awake by anxious thoughts. The boys continued to talk and joke for some time, until finally, their chatter died and gave way to heavy, drunken breathing.

It was a fact that there was no one to guide us, but beyond that, there was the threat of a future without meaning, hope, or purpose. Where could we go? We had very little access to education and no clear means to advance ourselves. In our old lives, we would have lived among the cattle and the clan. We would have been shepherds, as our fathers, grandfathers, and great grandfathers had been. There would have been a place for us and a role to play within the tribe. We would have had cattle, created families, participated in government and culture, stayed within our villages or, perhaps, moved to the city to get work or attend a university. In the refugee camp, nearly all of this seemed impossible. I wondered what would become of us.

Chapter Ten
THE SPIRIT SINGS

I waited in the food lines under the hot sun wishing things could move just a little bit faster. It was 1995 and I was nineteen years old. Most of my life had been as a refugee, and I was accustomed to waiting in lines, but the waits were getting longer and tensions among the people were growing. Yesterday, we waited all day and no food came. Today, it was late in the afternoon and still nothing. In the past weeks, the camp had doubled in size, reaching one hundred thousand. Originally, Kakuma was the official refugee camp for the South Sudanese, but now there were people from all over East Africa. When I arrived at the camp, we were mostly Lost Boys, but recently, entire groups, even families, came from Ethiopia, Rwanda, Somalia, Burundi, the Republic of Congo, and Uganda. The camp was brimful with people--a swarming mass of disease, thirst, and starvation.

"Get back in line and stay in line," a young Kenyan volunteer shouted, pushing a boy back into his place. There were dark sweat stains on his shirt, and he looked close to boiling over. "You people are like cows," he shouted, throwing his arms in the air with frustration. "You are worse than cows, at least cattle do what they are told," he sneered.

Many of us shook our heads at the insults, murmuring with indignation, but what could we do? We were so hungry we had to wait in the lines or starve. In the last months, it became clear that the volunteers and workers were overwhelmed by the stress and the sheer human need of the camp. Over the years, I had befriended many of them and knew their work was very challenging. They worked for six weeks and then took two weeks off, but lately, their jobs were so demanding that they were pushed to the breaking point. Mistrust mounted among us, and the food lines became a daily spectacle of humiliation and abuse. As I made my way closer to the front of the line, I overheard a worker yelling at a young girl.

"You can't take that much. What is wrong with you people?"

"I am trying to get food for my friend," the girl protested. "She is too sick to wait in line. This one is for me and this is for her."

The woman looked over at her fellow worker, manning the line with her. She rolled her eyes and shook her head in disgust, "Quit lying," she said harshly, grabbing the extra food from the girl. "Now go," she yelled, waving her out of sight.

I said nothing and looked away. I only wished there was something I could do. Hunger, waiting, and insults were a part of refugee life. An older man in front of me groaned in frustration and held his weary head in his hands. The girl could have easily been his daughter, and his rising anger was felt by all. Back in our village, he might have been a head clansman, but here we were treated like cattle, less than cattle, because we Jieng have always treated our cattle with great respect.

In time the clinic closed. People became sicker and sicker. You could hear babies cry, see young boys limping, and the elderly lying in the doorways of *tukuls*. Simply staring into space, they appeared to be waiting to die. There were several who found no shelter at all and water was scarce. Kakuma was more like Dimma every day. The school officially shut down. I would never get a high school degree as I had hoped.

Late one night by the dying fire, I took turns reading the New Testament with two other boys in my group. I listened to the rise and fall of my friend's voice as he read of how Jesus raised his friend Lazarus from the dead. I remembered Uncle Aluong's healing and how he became Paul, and I remembered Mother's face as she gave thanks for the miracle of his life.

"I have seen this," I said. "This happened, almost exactly like that, to my uncle Paul. He wasn't dead, but he was nearly dead."

"This is very good," my friend said, his voice hushed and reverent. I nodded in agreement, motioning for him to continue to read.

When I heard of the miracles that Christ performed, I was struck with how similar they were to what I had witnessed. The faith was much richer and broader than I had thought, and so very ancient. I learned that Jesus had been doing such things--miracles, giving life, making things new--for thousands of years. We read until the fires went out.

It was true that we had no school, but we did have Bibles, and we learned that they could teach us all we needed. My church had one New Testament for a few hundred, and I was charged with taking care of it. This was a great privilege. It was exciting to read as much Scripture as I wanted. I kept the Bible under my head at night and read it first thing in the morning as the sun was rising, and at night as the fire dwindled, I squinted in the dying light to make out the words. The Bible was my prized possession. I owned no other books. I didn't have classes, television, or the internet. The Bible and our stories as God's people were our major source for knowledge, information, and wisdom.

I read the Gospels and was astounded by the Gospel of John. I saw the glory of the Christ revealed in Baping, and it had been enough to sustain me for many years, but now I was growing in my faith and pressing deeper into God's Word. There seemed to always be more to learn. I learned more of who Jesus was and how he became incarnate, died, and was raised again. I learned that Jesus atoned for the sins of humanity. A new energy grew inside me that I had not felt since the days of burning down the shrines, when I danced by the red embers of the fire, watching with delight as the flames lit up the night. I recalled the feeling of excitement when Elijah preached, the rhythm of my drum, and the singing of the people. I soon discovered I was not alone in these feelings. Others were excited too.

I held my New Testament under my arm, making my way through the camp. "There is John with his Bible," a neighbor lady teased me. I smiled hello. Over many months, it became apparent to many that I was a pastor in training.

As I made my way to a clearing, I approached a gathering of five hundred refugees, assembled together under the trees and seated on makeshift mud benches. We called it "synagogue." We met every evening around five when the heat became more bearable. That night I was to lead us in the prayers. I made my way to the front and took my seat near some of the pastors. Our head minister, a Jieng, Anglican priest, stood up in the center of us all and made a cross over himself. He began our service with the ancient words, "Blessed be God, Father, Son, and Holy Spirit," and we the people responded in unison, "And blessed be his kingdom now and forever."

A young woman came to the front. All eyes were on her as she began to sing in a loud, beautifully clear voice. It filled us with a sweetness and beauty that we craved during the hard days of refugee life. I closed my eyes and lets the sounds wash over me, calming my soul. It was a new song, one that we had never heard, but the women in our gathering began to follow her lead, their voices rising and gaining strength. In time, the men joined in, and within minutes, we were all singing together. With five hundred voices rising, echoing through the camp, the sound and the witness could not be missed. Her song held a message of hope,

> The earth and the heavens are beautiful,
> All created and made by our God.
> Our suffering and misery are not eternal,
> But the beauty of the Lord endures forever.
> We will all be together in the New Jerusalem.
> Our families will be seated at the feet of Jesus,
> And there will be no more death.
> God will wipe away ever tear from our faces.

The potency of her message hit us with life and force. Our families and loved ones would be together yet again. It would be as it was in Baping, in those early days of the Christian fire. It would be as it was then, but better, stronger, and it would never end. We sang several songs together, pouring out our hearts to God as hope grew among us. We knew that there was more to life than this. This hardship was but a single moment in God's rich, unfolding plan for us.

As the afternoon sun faded into evening, the people dispersed to return to their dwellings or to find food. I felt lighter, with a buoyancy of spirit. I had never heard such beautiful music, and we didn't even have instruments that evening, just our voices. Not ready to return to my group, I remained with a group of pastors to chat about our church. These men and women often took me under their wing and instructed me. I learned so much from their wisdom and took every opportunity to talk and learn from them.

"The Spirit is pouring out songs upon us," said a church mother. She was short, with a sturdy frame and cheerful smile. Her enthusiasm spread, and we all nodded in agreement, for we all knew what she meant. God was speaking to us in a new, powerful way. As the difficulties of camp life grew, the presence of the Holy Spirit became even closer. Every time we came together to sing, it was as if our hearts were lifted to heaven and the songs kept coming. Every night a new person would be inspired and have a song.

"I believe God is saying things to us," said the Anglican priest. "It is as if he is training us, or showing us the Christian way in these stressful times. The songs are teaching us about him."

"All these songs," I said, "make me feel as if the words are spoken directly to us. God sees what is happening to us, and this is his answer." They murmured in unison. Something was different in our songs.

The true and most wonderful irony was that in the midst of our pitiful conditions, which seemed to be worsening every day, our spiritual life together was blossoming. We had found very little meaning in camp life, and so many years were lost, but I sensed a new spirit rising in the camp. We spent hours talking about God and what he was doing in our lives. As we shared in his suffering, I sensed Jesus was with us in a deeper and greater way, promising us the hope of his resurrection. I was not the only one who sensed this new movement, this new presence. People were becoming Christians in the camp with greater force. I felt a part of what had been lost was given back to us. We all wanted to know and experience more of this Jesus. He was changing everything.

The singing and the coming together was electric. The Holy Spirit was pouring out uncontainable energy through the songs. We did not have the whole Bible translated, we only had one copy of the New Testament, and we had very little teaching or instruction in the faith. Most of us were fairly new Christians, but God touched us. We had suffered for so long and we had grieved and doubted, but the Spirit understood and was speaking to our doubts and pain. We had cried out to God for many nights, and now he was answering us and the songs were his response.

At afternoon synagogue, a tall, slender boy came to the front. He reminded me of myself as a boy, young and tentative when I was tasked to preach the Gospel to my village. He was a little fellow, but his words had great power, and he began to sing with holy authority.

> Jesus is powerful and mighty.
> He is high on his throne and the devil has been cast out.
> Evil *jak,* you tormented us too long.
> We sacrificed our livelihood to you,
> But look at you now, evil *jak.*
> Look at you now!
> Jesus has defeated you!
> You have been conquered in the
> name of the Lord of Heaven!
> You have been cast out and cast down,
> No longer able to torment us.

"Hallelujah!" we exclaimed. "It is good and true," we shouted and began to join him in his chorus. Joy broke out among us as we moved and danced to the sounds of our own voices. God was with us, and he was more powerful than any force of evil against us. We danced to our rhythm and sang out for all to hear, "Jesus has defeated you!"

From the outside it appeared that we were losing--that all was hopeless, but we knew the truth. The truth was revealed in the songs. Christ's victory was our victory. We were conquering the evil of this world in the mighty name of Jesus who was with us, even in the dirt, disease, and despair of the Kakuma refugee camp. Jesus was with us, and we were his victors.

The songs took on a life and force of their own. The Holy Spirit sang the song to someone at night as they were falling asleep or during the day when they were in the food lines. The person would begin to teach it to the others, singing it to them. They would find their church leader and sing it to him. The leader sang it back as if he were a tape recorder, memorizing the words. They took the song and edited it, making sure it contained nothing they knew to be contrary to Scripture. Then the leader taught the songs to all the worshipers at evening prayer. This was the main thing we did at synagogue, learn and sing the Spirit's songs together. Eventually, there were so many songs we designated a few people to work as guides, checking the songs to see how they fit with the Scriptures. We sang from five to eight in the evening every night. Our voices were heard by all. They filled the camp with our singing; every ear could hear us. We were singing, three to four hundred people in one gathering, learning the songs one after another.

The songs were our primary means of discipleship. They conveyed spiritual truths and instructed us into the nature of the Christian life. The songs were often given to individuals who had little knowledge of the Bible, or education in general, but they wrote theologically sophisticated and complex songs of seven or eight stanzas that mirrored biblical ideas. They were a means of informing the people of the truth of Jesus, and his power to heal, save, and love them. Sometimes the songs were given to boys, sometimes to girls, or to men and women, young and old. Sometimes they were given to experienced pastors or to the newly baptized. It didn't matter. God never discriminated.

These songs were born in the context of suffering, death, insults, and mockery. They came out of places of intense sorrow and uncertainty. Many of the songs took on the form of lamenting, echoing the laments found in Scripture such as in Isaiah 18 or Psalm 79.

REV. JOHN CHOL DAAU AND LILLY SANDERS UBBENS

An injured man limped to the front of our gathering. He was physically weak and his voice was not particularly beautiful, but at once we understood his words and were soon singing with him.

> How long, Oh Lord?
> Will you be angry forever?
> How long will you keep us away from our land?
> How long must we be hated by foreigners?
> How long will we be kept like animals?
> How long must we be feeding from the hands of others?
> How long will we be food for the birds and the wild animals?
> We don't have our mothers and fathers.
> We have lost our sisters and brothers.
> We are orphans without land.

This man had lost his identity, family, and status, but his words gave us hope to go forward. We could all relate to his words and we understood his pain. We sang songs that recounted our suffering and affirmed our faith.

> Thank you my Father, the living God, for the
> work you have done for us worldwide.
> Lord, it was your gift; it was a gift you prepared.
> You sent us the Atoning Lamb of your
> own work while no one knew it.
> It was you who knew it, the only
> One who sent him to us.
> He was born in our nature and laughed
> like us, as human beings.
> He came and suffered in our sins on the cross as well.

Trinity, save our souls for they are crawling to fire.
Everybody has gathered before you, praying for souls.
Are you not with power on earth? you created human beings from the dust of ground, and breathed life into him and he lives by himself.
Our souls are in agony for the world is
sweeping us off, O God of life.

Everybody, don't believe with wavering faith,
because God doesn't give up on us.
He loves people in this world.
Just pray to him wherever you are--even
under the tree in the bush, pray!
Our God doesn't get tired of human beings
whom he created in his image.
Please grant us peace and love, Lord Christ.
Let the Holy Spirit come in us and dwell in us forever.

My father and my mother, lean on the Lord
My brother and my sister, lean on the Lord.
Come all of you and follow the way,
The good way of the Lamb where we were
cleansed with his precious blood.
What are you waiting for?
We heard in the Bible that the earth will be destroyed.
Its destruction will come like a thief,
so everybody should get ready.
The Son of Man will come gloriously, accompanied by angels with the sound of trumpets.
Will you stand it?

> It is only you, Jehovah, I lean on.
> Let me not be ashamed, save me by your righteousness.
> Have mercy on me, O Giver of all good.
> It is being read here, but we don't seem
> to get it as the only truth.
> Have mercy Lord for your chosen peo-
> ple and grant us light to save us.
> You have promised to us the Bible as a
> path and life, but we don't listen to it.
> O God, help us forever![8]

My soul had crawled through the fire for years and I had work so hard to survive, to keep my heartbreak at bay, but with these songs, the floodgates of my soul were finally released. I would say that it was there, under the trees, singing those Spirit-given songs with my fellow Christians, that I finally allowed my heart to break, giving it to God to make it into something new.

---

[8] This untitled song, written and translated by Rev. Samuel Galuak Marial, was authored in 1993 in the Kakuma Refugee Camp, after personal tragedy. In his words, "The lord was my source of recovery from the loss of my brother and mother. He pointed me to pick up life again and strengthened me to ascend the stairs of my Christian faith. It was at this time I began to count only on him. He restored my hope, and I began to thank him in a number of songs which I wrote to send forth Jesus Christ to save the world, bringing salvation which came with joy to those who would never have a chance to feel joy for life like I do." Trinity School for Ministy, Ambridge, PA. March, 2011.

Chapter Eleven

TAKEN

It was the first time I had ever received money. I stood in the International Organization of Migration's headquarters, gripping the hard Kenyan coins in my hand, discovering their feel. It wasn't much, not even a U.S. dollar, but it was something, a beginning. Perhaps with this small salary, I could enroll in a class one day. After handing me my pay, a young American man who worked there smiled at me and shook my hand.

"We are happy to have you working for us, John. Do you enjoy the translation work?" I had begun working at the IOM because they needed English translators and my solid English language education granted me the position.

"Oh, yes, very much," I said. Recently I had been translating short seminars for refugees who qualified for scholarships in the United States. The IOM was involved in helping refugees to find places to settle and advance themselves.

"Have you ever thought about going to the United States?" he asked.

"I never thought I would have the opportunity," I said, stunned by his question.

"We are all impressed with your work ethic," he said. "You should try and apply."

Something about immigrating to the United States troubled me. How could I leave my people? What if the war finally ended and I missed the opportunity to return to my homeland? I considered his words carefully.

"What do you think I could do" I asked, hesitating, "if I could leave?"

"What would you like to do?" he responded.

"Receive an education." The words readily spilled out. I didn't even have to think about it. That dream had been there for so long, always unspoken.

"I think with the right scholarship, this he could be possible," he said. A pang of hope coursed through me. "Maybe this is my chance," I thought. "Maybe this is God's call on my life, my purpose." Jolted by this young man's words, I decided to apply. I stayed at the office for some time, filling out the necessary paper work. As I began the scholarship process, I couldn't help but feel that things might be changing for me.

I knelt on the dusty ground clutching my Prayer Book as the wind rustled its pages. It had been months since I had heard any news of my scholarship to immigrate, and I was troubled, but as I led Morning Prayer with a small gathering of brothers and sisters under the warm, Kenyan sun, strength rose within me. There was a moment of silent intercession, and a prayer welled up in me. "Lord, what are you doing with my life? Why have I gone through all this? How long, Jesus, will I be here? Will I become an old man in the camp?" These were not new prayers, lately they were always on my mind and heart. When I looked toward my future, I saw the futility of camp life stretching before me. I was beginning to think that my life would never change, and wondered if I would ever get out of the camp. I was a young man, in my early twenties, and my spirit was aching for some greater purpose and work.

Rising from the ground, I read aloud, "Let us bless the Lord." They replied in unison, "Thanks be to God."

We parted ways and the people went on their daily tasks and errands. I dusted the dirt off my pants and decided to walk toward the Red Cross message board to see if there was any news of friends or family. The board had lists and lists of refugees' names, the camps they were in, and whether they were dead or alive. These lists were regularly updated and distributed throughout refugee camps in East Africa. There was always a crowd of people around the lists, trying to gather news of lost loved ones and friends. I, along with many others, sometimes spent hours looking through the lists trying to find names we recognized.

When I first arrived at Kakuma, I learned my father was dead. I was not shocked. Somehow, I had always known that he, like so many of the fighting age men, was killed in the invasion of our village. I still hoped for the others--Joseph, Mother, Paul, and Elijah. I wondered and prayed for them, imagining our reunion after so many years. Perhaps Elijah was still planting churches. Joseph had always been very bright. Maybe he became one of the lucky few who received an education. Had he carried on with Jesus after all these years? I wondered if he was now my height. It was hard to picture him as anything other than a small boy. He was, as many in the village said, my younger twin. We had been inseparable. With Mother, it was harder to imagine what became of her. I knew that many young women were captured, sent up North, and sold into slavery, or they were killed in the violence of war. Unspeakable things were done to sisters and mothers in this war. Others in the trek died from hunger, thirst, gunshot wounds, or disease. If Mother had lived, it was hard for me to picture her life. I could only hope she was safe somewhere in a camp, but I knew that if she were alive, she was in constant grief for her family. What if she had been reunited with Joseph? What a wonderful thought.

That morning, I searched through the names, tracing through them with my finger and taking my time, moving slowly. If I went too quickly over a name, I might miss something, and all the long hours of looking would be lost. I froze when I saw it. "If you are John Chol Madioor Daau..." it read. I inhaled sharply, shocked to read my mother's name--Tabitha Nyaluak Madior. The letters stood out boldly on the page. I could not be dreaming. I realized that I was holding my breath, and my hands were shaking. I read the message one more time and then again. Her message had been sent two years ago. She was alive and living in a displaced camp on the Southern Sudan and Ugandan border. A prayer that on certain nights I had been too fearful to voice had been answered. My mother was alive! It had been over eleven years since I had seen her on the morning of the invasion. She had fed me milk and I remembered how she looked, her smile and her calling goodbye to me as I walked to the cattle camp. The washing clutched in her hands. After years of never knowing and only hoping, she was alive! "Mother," I whispered to myself. I couldn't quite believe it, but I decided to leave for Uganda that day.

I traveled for days until I reached Mother's camp in Mogali. I had so many questions for her. I wondered what her life had been like, how she had escaped the invasion, and if she had been in the camps this entire time. I hoped she knew of the others.

The camp at Mogali was much different from Kakuma. There were fewer *tukuls* and the place was less crowded and dusty. Mogali was not a refugee camp, but a camp for displaced persons. When the war had escalated between 1988 and 1995 and most villagers were forced out, nearly all of the Jieng people became displaced in the process. It made me think that Mother had become a part of this trek and had survived in the Ugandan camps for years. I went to the headquarters to check with the officials to see if she was registered.

"Hello, I am looking for Tabitha Nyaluak Madior. I am her son. We have been separated for nearly twelve years. I recently found that she sent a message for me through the Red Cross, and I believe that she is living in this camp."

The man nodded his head perfunctorily, as if he had heard this type of story countless times before. He left to check his rosters. I waited for him to return. My heart was racing. I was so excited. I couldn't believe I was this close to being reunited with family. Over an hour passed before the man in charge returned with a solemn expression.

"We no longer have her in our camp roster," he said. "That doesn't mean she is no longer at the camp." He seemed to stress these words. "But, we no longer have her on file. She could still be here or she might have moved to a different camp." His words were direct and to the point. All my dreams of reunion fell away. I looked down at the concrete slab floor of the office and wondered what to do next.

"How might I find her?" I asked. "I mean, do you have any advice? Do you think she is still here?"

He shrugged. "It's possible," he said. "You'll simply have to search for her."

"How many people are in this camp?" I asked.

"Over forty thousand," the man said, raising his hands as if to say that there was nothing he could do for me.

What were the chances of finding one person out of forty thousand? How could I possibly search every *tukul* for her? Part of me was furious. I wanted to throw his files over the counter and storm through the camp in a rage, but I hurriedly thanked him and dashed out of the office.

It was brutally hot. I sat down on my heels and leaned against the concrete building to steady myself, clasping my hands tightly in frustration. I tried to think straight, but my head was spinning with ideas. What was I thinking to get so excited? I should have known better than to let my dreams run away with me. I should turn around and go back to Kakuma. I'll never find her here. What if she is dead? Thousands of people die in the camps. I crouched there in the heat, angry and confused. I knew that the chances of my finding her were next to nothing, but in my heart, I still hoped and believed. Who knew, perhaps she was right down the road. I prayed silently. God had brought me here for a reason. I couldn't just give up.

I rose and, wasting no time, began my search. I went from *tukul* to *tukul*, greeting people, asking if they knew or had heard of my mother. I got many sympathetic responses, "Sorry, we haven't," they said. "Check back with us. We will spread the word."

I became more and more despondent. My hope to reunite with her had consumed me. I loved her, she was my family, and I longed to have family again. I was tempted to turn back but decided to push forward.

After hours of searching for her in the heat without food or water, I was exhausted. As I walked along, I heard singing and prayers in the camp, and I knew there were Christians nearby. I followed the sound, making my way to a group of worshipers. An Anglican priest stood in the center of the group, preaching a sermon for all to hear. "Perhaps he could help me," I thought. I sat among the Christians and joined in their songs and worship, letting myself finally rest from what had been hours of walking. My clothes were damp with sweat and my shoes covered in dirt, but when I looked around, I noticed that many were in worse shape. Almost all were barefoot, several without clothing. They seemed hungry and tired. When the service ended, I introduced myself to the priest.

"Hello, my name is John," I said. "I am a Christian and I have traveled here from the Kakuma camp in Kenya in search of my mother, Tabitha Nyaluak Madior. I am wondering if you know her? He looked at me and paused in thought. He was a pastor to so many. He was trying to remember them all.

"I don't believe we do," he said and extended his hand toward me. "I am the Rev. Phillip Jok Kuol," he said with a friendly smile. "John you are welcome here as our brother. Do you need some food and water?"

I nodded in great relief. That evening Rev. Phillip, along with a few other church members, invited me in and gave me food and water. I could tell they had very little and I felt bad taking a small portion of their beans, but after days of walking, I devoured them in spite of myself. Sitting outside his *tukul*, we talked for some time about my work in the church and my journey from Baping.

"Have you been looking for your family all this time?" he asked.

"Oh yes, for eleven years now we have been separated. I know my father died in the invasion, but I always hoped for the others. When I got the word about my mother, I can't describe how happy I was."

He murmured kindheartedly; he had searched for family too. "What do you think you will do now, John?" he asked.

"I don't want to return to Kakuma," I said. I was surprised by how strongly I felt those words. I was tired of Kakuma and I hated the idea of going back to an empty future without family. "What if she is here close by and I miss her?" I continued. "This is my only chance at reunion."

Rev. Phillip nodded his head in agreement. "You are welcome to stay here with us for as long as you need to, John. You will see that there is much to be done here. We could use someone like you, but I should warn you things are not easy here. Our life here is very difficult. People are dying daily." There was a gravity to his tone, and I knew that he had lost many people.

That morning I went with Rev. Phillip on his pastoral rounds. I quickly saw that his words were true. Of all the camps I had seen, I had never witnessed suffering like that of Mogali. Children were starving, and their mothers were racked with hysteria. I was in awe of Rev. Phillip and the care he showed them. The people were so desperate, hoping he could help them in some way. The first mother we visited clutched his hands in hers as she desperately explained her situation.

"We have not eaten in so long," she said. "My children are wasting away."

He managed to remain at peace, sitting beside her, listening patiently, and praying for her. "We can send some church mothers to you," he said. "They have very little food, but we might have something to spare."

She wept on his shoulder, great sobs racking her body. Her children sat at her feet with swollen bellies. It was a painful place, but Rev. Phillip continued to remind her of the promises of Jesus and his great love for his people. The situation in Mogali was more desperate than I had realized, and to think, Mother had existed here this whole time.

Rev. Phillip was overwhelmed by his church responsibilities. He put me in charge of youth ministry and offered to help mentor me in my work as long as I stayed. A large part of my duties was collecting songs, along with teaching, Scripture reading, and preaching. In Mogali there was a sea of new Christians and very few seasoned Christian leaders. I was amazed by the number of churches in Mogali. It made me believe that the spiritual awakening that was happening in Kakuma was happening over all of East Africa. I was commissioned as an evangelist at the age of seventeen, so I found myself in a position to help to my brothers and sisters. [9] They were all new Christians and had many unanswered questions.

---

9 Most of the Anglican churches in East Africa have a system of commissioning lay ministers to assist in the duties of the church: preaching, teaching, assisting in baptism, and preaching. There was a great need for Christian leaders since the growth church growth was so overwhelming that the ordained clergy were desperate for help.

The work was engrossing, and I found a wonderful community there. God gave me, for the first time since my days with Uncle Eljiah, a mentor. Rather than treating me like a young church leader, Rev. Phillip treated me like a son. He was attentive to my potential, and he instructed me church activities as well as life in general. He told me core things about life and truth. Not having had any parental guidance in years, I soaked in his wisdom. He often told me, "When you preach God's Word, and you will, you must only have one thing to say. Find out what God wants you to say and say it. Don't just talk."

I noticed that Rev. Phillip always carried his Bible everywhere and handled it with care. He told me, "We never know when we will have to run away again, but if you have to run, don't forget your Bible. Cling to your Bible always. It will see you through."

He impressed on me a deep love of Scripture which I never forgot. Although it was a terribly sad place, and I was on a quest to find my mother, I still found peace in the ministry and working alongside Rev. Phillip.

As the sun was beginning to rise in the east, I woke early to begin my daily search. Over the past few weeks, I had developed a routine of walking through designated areas, inquiring after Mother, careful not to repeat my steps. I searched in the morning, and then went on my ministry rounds. When the day was winding down, I picked up where I had left off. In a few weeks, I had visited only a small portion of the camp. That I afternoon, I stopped to speak with a young man and his wife,

"Hello," I said, "I am looking for Tabitha…" A thundering roar ripped through the sky and, far to the left of me, I saw dirt exploding in the air.

"Run!" the young man yelled, grabbing his wife and baby.

I took off, running with them, disoriented by the sounds of explosions. In the distance, I heard bombs exploding, screams echoed through the camp.

"Get down!" someone shouted, pulling me down to the ground with him. The bombs were nearer now. I hugged the earth, covering my head with my hands. I crouched there, my face pressed into the dirt, trembling with the impact of each bomb, until at last the sounds stopped. I was shaking, my knees unable to bend. "What is happening?" I thought. I heard the injured weeping and wailing, but my ears were so deafened from the explosions that their cries sounded eerily distant and surreal. I checked my body, everything was intact.

I began running back to the church. "What was that?" I thought. "Will we have to run again? Is someone coming after us?"

Rev. Phillip's words rang through my mind, "Always carry your Bible. You never know when you'll have to run."

I couldn't fathom who would attack a camp of displaced persons. People around me were scared, cowering in their *tukuls*, grasping hold of each other, assessing their wounds. A mother held her baby tightly to her chest and wept, but nobody was running. Had this happened before?

Rev. Phillip was at the church, along with a small gathering of Christians, but more were coming even as I arrived. I was glad to see that he appeared well and was in one piece.

"What was that?" I asked, still dazed from the explosions.

"Has this never happened in Kakuma?" he asked solemnly. "It is a tactic of the Northern government. They air raid us to keep us afraid, to secure their power."

I plopped down beside him, lost for words, still trembling from the blows. As the church began to fill, Rev. Phillip knelt before the people and began to pray silently. Others joined, some calling out in sorrow, voicing their anguish to God. What else could they do in this world of terror? We waited to hear news of how many people had died, but so far, we had heard nothing. We were visibly afraid. We didn't want to separate at that moment. We weren't sure if it would happen again. Was Mother alive? Did she witness the raid? Gathered together in our under-tree church with no walls, it suddenly felt like a prison.

Over the next few days, the pastors met together to pray for the people. Despite the recent scare, the spiritual hunger was strong. People needed the courage and hope of Christ. They were desperate without it.

"I think we should hold a "Witness for the Week Campaign,"" a young pastor suggested to the group of us. This had been done before in the camp. It was a way to spread the good news of Jesus to the people.

"We shouldn't wait," a church mother said. "The people need this. It is their only comfort."

For the "Witness for the Week," we evangelized all day and into the evening for an entire week going door to door.[10] The church leaders divided into smaller groups with many men and women coming to minister with them. My group walked the camp, seen by all, carrying our crosses and Bibles. We visited friends who had not been to church in a long time, the starving, and the sick. We sometimes stopped to have impromptu worship in their *tukuls,* praying for God to bless and strengthen them.

On the last day, as our witness was coming to a close, a young woman came running after us with her child who was very sick.

---

10 This was a practice that they had heard was done in the North. When Christianity was outlawed there, the Christians would meet in each other's houses and eventually, they would share the love of Christ with their neighbors. It was a practice the Southerners were replicating, especially now that they were in the more pluralistic world of the camps which had multiple faiths and tribes.

Sallow and emaciated, the mother didn't look much older than a girl herself. The child had been sick for nearly a week and could barely breathe. It was a time of severe malnutrition in the displaced camp. Food was so scarce that people were dying of starvation. They had nothing to eat, nothing to get from their mothers to breasts, because their mothers were not eating well themselves. There was one little clinic for forty thousand people, run by the Diocese of Torit, a Catholic diocese.

This young woman and her baby were lost in this place of suffering, and they were between life and death. She found me and the others worshiping and stopped us. She feebly grasped my arm and held her little baby close to her heart. "I want you people to pray for my child. I know she is going to die, but I want you to pray for her. She has been very sick for more than a week. Now she can barely breathe. I believe God can heal her, but if he doesn't, I won't be angry with him."

Tears were streaming down her face as she appeared resigned to a miserable fate. She handed her daughter to a woman in our group and fell to her knees weeping. A church mother came beside her and held her as she wept. We immediately stopped what we were doing and surrounded her and the baby. The baby's breath was low and shallow. She was tiny, shrunken from starvation.

We placed her in her mother's arms and I watched as she gazed at her child with love and sorrow. We all circled her and laid hands on the baby and prayed. "In the mighty name of Jesus Christ you are to be healed," I prayed, my voice trembling.

We sat and prayed in silence for some time. At last, the baby opened her eyes and was able to breast feed. The child was healed. We took the baby and mother with us to a place where we knew there was food. The mother was crying so hard we had to help feed her. The church mothers held her up, spooning the beans into her mouth between her sobs. She was overcome with joy and relief.

It wasn't until I met with all the other evangelists that I understood the full scope of what God was doing. At least a hundred people had been healed during our week-long door to door worship. Many had come to Christ. Paul Majok and Daniel Deng baptized more than eight hundred people in one week.[11] It was amazing! The energy could be felt everywhere. Even at my little church of three hundred, considered little because most of the churches had five hundred or more members, there were no fewer than seventy new people who were baptized during that week. I wasn't surprised by the miracles. From my own birth, to my uncle Paul's healing, and to all the times I had escaped from death, I simply knew that God did miracles. When hundreds of reports came in of healings and exorcisms, I thought of how God had always acted to save his people. He always showed us mercy. He always helped us in our times of great need and there had been many such times.

I grew to love my ministry in Mogali, but it was also a place of deep sadness. I looked tirelessly for Mother, searching through countless *tukuls*. I didn't know what had happened to her. She could be anywhere, even dead. That was my greatest fear. Perhaps she had died, like so many in the camp, from hunger or disease.

I could not bear returning to Kakuma without her. I prayed that I would be reunited with her during my stay, and I believed that God had brought me there for this purpose. I was confused and couldn't bear to face Kakuma again, but I knew my time in Mogali was coming to an end. I needed to return to Kakuma, if for no other reason than to check on my scholarship. The last time

---

11 The Most Rev. Daniel Deng is now Archbishop of the Episcopal Church of Sudan.

I had spoken with IOM, they were optimistic about my chances. Perhaps by now word had come through. If I could check on my scholarship, then in a few weeks I might be able to return to look for Mother. Perhaps, by then, word of my search would have reached her.

Rev. Phillip and a few others saw me off from the camp. "John, we will miss you. You have been like a son to me," he said. "I pray that God will continue to bless your life."

I was touched by his words and hoped that I could live the kind of life that would make him proud, but in truth, I had no idea what the future held.

When I returned to Kakuma, the news of September eleventh had just reached us. I was shocked by what had happened to the World Trade Center Towers in New York City. I knew what it was like to have one's homeland invaded and loved ones killed. We prayed for our brothers and sisters in America, that God would bless them during this time.

I went to check on my friends at the IOM. They were very busy. What had occurred in America had changed everything for them. I saw my friend. He was, as always, working tirelessly. "Hello, John," he said.

"I am so sorry for what has happened in your homeland," I said.

He nodded and rubbed his forehead in fatigue. "Thank you," he said softly. "John, I'm afraid I have bad news. After what happened on September eleventh, the United States is no longer giving scholarships to immigrate, and most likely, it won't be able to for some time. I'm sorry, John. It looks like you won't be able to leave or get that education. You deserved it, John. I'm really sorry."

My last hope was dashed. Three of the things I had cared for most, my family, the possibility of a life outside the camp, and an education, had been taken

Chapter Twelve

THROWN AWAY

"**H**ey, John, we are ready for synagogue. Are you coming with us?" Two of my friends from church stood by my *tukul* waiting for me.

I shook my head no. They shrugged and walked away. It had been over two weeks since I had met with other Christians. I sat around listlessly under the trees, going along with the talking and joking of the boys in my group. Sometimes I played soccer. At other times, I stared into space and dreamed of things that could never be.

"Why are you not going, John?" one of them asked me in surprise. "You always go, don't you?"

I smiled half-heartedly and shook my head as if I didn't care. "Not always," I said. The truth was, I no longer had the same passion, and my heart was bitter within me. I didn't care anymore for the prayers, the singing, any of it. How long I had called out to God and asked him to change my life? There seemed to be nothing for me. I sat in the afternoon sun, listening to the other boys in my group as they chatted and carried on with bravado.

"You should see what the girls look like in Nairobi, John." One said to me. "There is so much to do there. Last night we stayed out all night."

Something about their talked made me uneasy. I knew Elijah would not approve, but I quickly pushed the thought aside. There was something about their confidence, their easy tone, which appealed to me. They seemed to have no cares in the world. Things came naturally to them. It was as if they were going places and doing things. All I knew was life inside the camp. These boys appeared to be unafraid, as if they could do whatever they wanted.

"Have you ever had a girlfriend, John?" one of them asked me.

I shook my head no, shyness creeping over me. I quickly looked away at the boys playing soccer in the distance, not wanting to meet their gaze. I knew these boys were very experienced with such things. Now that I was a young man, I knew that I wanted to be with a young woman, but I had no idea how to go about it.

Since I was a boy, it had always been assumed that my wife would be chosen from among the clan. I would have some say in it, of course, and so would she, but the whole marriage would be mediated through our families. It was always the boy's father who spoke to the bride's family and worked out the dowry price. This custom had continued, as best it could, even during the wartime, but I had no family to speak for me or to show me how to marry. I was very naïve and without guidance.

"Well, let us know when you want one," he said. They all began to snicker as if they shared some great secret. "We can get you a girlfriend, no problem."

At this, they all began to laugh loudly and elbowed each other good naturedly. I was embarrassed at my own ignorance, but I smiled to hide it. They all slapped me on the back as if we were long-time friends. Somewhere inside myself, I wondered what I was doing with these boys. I had never entertained their jokes before. In the past, I had been frustrated with their petty chatter, but something had changed and I couldn't even say what it was.

I had never had a girlfriend, and I was desperately lonely. I loved being with her. I was no longer alone and hopeless. After a few dates, I was sure I wanted to marry her. I knew, however, that I was going about it in the wrong way. But this was the first time in years that I didn't feel alone. I was far from God, with a heart that had the scars of a lost future. After a short period of knowing her, she came to me in the night to tell me she expected a child, and that the baby was mine.

In Jieng culture if a woman is unmarried and pregnant, she will go to the baby's father in the nighttime, sneaking away from her home so no one will notice. She will then tell him of her condition, and he has the choice to either reject or accept her.[12] I loved this young woman and proposed to her immediately.

The idea of being a father was an amazing revelation. We would be a family together, but I knew that I had sinned by not marrying her first. I felt ashamed of my sin, but despite this failure, I was eager to be a husband and father. Yes, I had sinned, but God could bring good out of this, and I would work to do all I could to have a loving family.

I knew that the right thing to do was to go back to the church. With my priest, I went through the rite of repentance and reconciliation. I received counseling from the church elders. I knew I had failed the church and this woman, but I wanted to put it all to right and have a life with her and our child. It was the desire of my heart to be married. I arranged it with a priest in the church that we could be married after he counseled with us. It was one of the greatest days of my life. I then knew I had to arrange it with her family, which would prove to be difficult, much more difficult than I could have anticipated.

---

12 According to Jieng law, custody rights are given to the men. If the man refuses to marry the woman, he must go to the village court and pay a penalty fine. The woman will return to her parents, and the man will then either relinquish custody of the child to her and her family, or he will pay a sum of money to receive custody of the child.

According to Jieng custom, marriages are arranged through families, and the man is expected to pay a dowry to marry a woman. The dowry is normally paid in cattle, livestock, or other gifts. These things are always worked out among families, but I had no family to negotiate a marriage or the cost of the dowry, and as a refugee I had no money to pay it. The little salary I had saved wasn't even close to what I needed. Deeply afraid of what they might think, I arranged a meeting with her family.

My bride-to-be and I arrived together at her house. When we entered the *tukul*, I knew immediately that something was very wrong. Her family sat together in a circle and looked at me with hostile eyes. I prayed to God for strength. I explained my intentions. They were instantly furious with me and their daughter. Women in Jieng culture are prized for their ability to secure a dowry, and it is a point of pride and status for a young women. Her father arose from his seat and waved his hands at his daughter violently, then shook her by the shoulders.[13]

"Look what you've done. You have thrown yourself on this man who is nothing. He is garbage. He doesn't even have someone to speak for him."

"Sir, please," I summoned my courage. "I am a pastor at a church and I should have known better. I made a mistake. It is entirely my fault."

He pointed at me in a rage. "Who are you to talk to me of this? You have no one here to speak for you."

My bride crumpled to the floor in sorrow and began to wail. I felt tears come to my eyes and a panic I had never felt before, not

---

[13] The negotiation system is very elaborate. Everyone in the family should have something to say, and those without family are looked down upon. The fact that John had no one to speak for him was scandalous in the eyes of his fiancé's parents.

in all my years of running from hostile soldiers. I had never felt so afraid as in that moment.

"Sir, I have talked with my church elders. They say we are forgiven by Jesus Christ, and will marry us with your permission. I do not have much to offer now, but I will one day. I greatly want to marry your daughter and provide for her and our child in the best way I can."

He looked at me, his face hard and assessing. His eldest son stood beside him and began to hurl insults at me. "You are stupid, garbage. If you can't bring us a dowry, you cannot marry her."

"I will pay it in time," I said. "I will pay it all in time." I could hear the tears in my voice and was ashamed, but it was a promise that I was determined to keep. I hoped that if I could persuade the family that I was honest and trustworthy, they would change their minds. I couldn't blame them for their anger. I had gotten us into a terrible situation, but I really wanted to make it right. I stood in the middle of the room, trying not to run away. I wanted it right so badly. The brothers circled around me, their faces hot and menacing. My bride sat bent over in the corner of the room along with the other women, watching helplessly.

"How can you pay it?" the father demanded. His face was inches away from mine, his chest heaving with rage. "You have no family to help you," he hissed. "You have no land or cattle of your own." The father was certain that without my having a family, I would never have the resources to pay the dowry.[14]

---

14 Many young men are only able to pay dowries after their own sisters have been married and their families have received her bride price. Without the dowry of a sister, marriage within Jieng custom is extremely difficult, yet another reason why John's not having a family diminished him in their eyes.

"I can speak English," I said desperately. "I could teach. I could go to school. I could move to America or Australia where there are work opportunities for people like me."

Suddenly, the Father swung at me. The blow to my face sent me reeling. At once, the brothers were pinning me to the ground where they continued to rough me up. My head throbbed and a loud ringing stormed through my head.

"You have gotten away easy," a brother shouted in my face. "If you ever try to come back here again, it will be much worse."

They threw me out of the door, and as I was doubled over on the ground, I could see my bride standing in the doorway. Her hands covered her eyes and she was sobbing. I had ruined her life.

That night I told no one what had happened. I didn't return to my *tukul* because I never wanted to see those boys again. I spent the night alone, at the edge of the camp. I listened to the night breezes and the sounds of distant animals, people coming and going, calling to each other. All the camp fires had gone out, and there was only blackness. I wanted to pray to God. I wanted nothing more than to tell him how sorry I was, but I wondered if he would even want to hear me, if I even deserved to call on him. I had thought that my life was for nothing and that this was God's fault, but now I knew who was wrong--it was me. I had learned in a few short days just how bad I could be. I never thought I would ruin someone's life, but I had.

Despite their threats, I often went to her house and stood outside her compound for hours, hoping to speak with her, to tell her how sorry I was, and how I had planned to marry her. Her family would come out, shouting at me, and threatening me with violence if I didn't leave. Still I would come back, bringing a small gift or token for the unborn child whom I feared I would never see.

One day her brother came to the door. He met me where I was waiting and looked me over, not saying anything. For a moment,

I was hopeful. I thought perhaps I had won them over, that they had changed their minds.

"It has been arranged that she is to be married to someone else. The marriage should happen very soon," her brother said. "This man will raise her child and you are to have nothing to do with them."

I stood perfectly still, slowly taking in what I had just heard. The words killed me. The brother turned abruptly and returned to the family compound. I wanted to speak, but there was nothing to say. I felt as if absolutely everything was gone from me. I imagined the little baby whom I would never hold, never see.

I appealed to the village court. If I could raise the money to pay a penalty for not marrying this woman with the proper dowry fee, I could be free to raise my child or at least, share in his upbringing. The fee was nearly 800 U.S. dollars, a staggering fee. How could I possibly ever raise the money to see my child?

I went back to Kakuma with no energy or hope for the future. The thing I most needed now was to return to my church and to God's people. I hoped they would embrace me again as my only family, but I was ashamed of myself and feared their judgment. My wife and baby were gone. I knew now that I would never be a priest. I didn't feel worthy of it. I didn't feel worthy of anything.

Chapter Thirteen
THIS IS GOD!

We sat outside his *tukul* on a clear afternoon, drinking strong coffee from rusted tin cups. "Where have you been all this time, John? We have missed you."

The seasoned pastor, whom I had come to love and respect, leaned forward on his bench, his expression warm and attentive. I squirmed slightly under his caring gaze. Confused and humiliated, I had been wandering in out of the camp for weeks, sleeping here and there. I couldn't bring myself to return to my group and face the crowd of boys who had introduced me to her. It wasn't their fault. I knew it was mine alone, but it was just too painful to return. For weeks now I had avoided everyone I knew or cared about. I couldn't face them. I was too ashamed. It had taken me days of building the courage to visit one of my old mentors. He placed a firm hand on my shoulder.

"You are my son, John. You are our family. We don't want to see you go."

I broke down at his kindness and the words tumbled out of me as I told him the whole story. He listened quietly, thinking and praying as I talked and talked. Even as I was confessing, I could feel a great weight being lifted off my chest.

I thought for a moment, staring up at the clear blue sky, the warm sun shining down on us. The best thing that any of us can learn is that we are not worthy of Jesus. For us to follow Jesus we must know how much we need him, that we are the sinful ones. It is easy to blame everyone else, but it isn't God, it isn't the government, the Muslims, the volunteers, or any of it. It is us. We are the sinners.

My first lesson on sin sprung to mind. I remembered how I watched the boys mistreating each other at the cattle camp and ran back to Elijah that same night. "I have seen sin," I had told him proudly. I had meant that sin was in the world, but what about in me? "You will see even more than this," had been his words. He was right. I hadn't just seen sin--now I had known it personally. It wasn't just out there, but in me, and it came with great consequences. I placed my head in my hands and let the feelings of contrition wash over me.

"Everyone can be forgiven by God, and it is those of us who are forgiven much that much will be required. We all think that there is a call on your life, John. Perhaps this is part of it."

I listened to the pastor's counsel carefully and realized I had a choice. I could further isolate myself, perhaps even go to another refugee camp, or return to my Christian community and accept God's forgiveness.

That Sunday, I went back to church under the trees. My throat was dry and my heart was pounding in my chest. "What would I say to them?" I wondered. "What would they think of me?"

In the early morning light a group of young people stood by the trees, talking and laughing, waiting for the service to begin. A young man looked at me, his face alight with a smile. "Our brother is back!" he shouted loudly for all to hear.

Relief pulsed through me, along with the spontaneous joy of being accepted. "We missed you John," a young woman said. They came to me and hugged me one by one. "You must sit with us today, John. We have so much to tell you. You have missed many good songs and teaching." I sat down between my brothers and sisters. They said we were family, and this time I believed them.

We began to sing our songs. There were many new ones I didn't know, and others that were familiar to me. As our voices lifted, I felt the Holy Spirit embrace me again, as if I were his long lost son. Jesus was welcoming me back into his family, but this time I didn't run from him. Where else could I go? I realized now that it was God alone who sustained me all these years, running in the bush, through bullets, through hunger, thirst, and disease. He sustained me even through my own sin and heartbreak. He was there with me, and he alone gave me life. All these years, I had been looking for family and home when right here I had both. Most of all, I had a Father who loved me and would not abandon me. That day, with the voices of my brothers and sisters circling around me and the breath of the Holy Spirit on my soul, I surrendered all I had to Jesus. Even if that meant I would grow old and die in the Kakuma Refugee Camp, I would be with my Father.

After the service ended, we all stood under the trees and chatted. I saw a young man running toward me, smiling and waving, and I recognized him immediately as a distant relative from Baping. The boy was just a little younger than I was. Such reunions were rare and came with great hope of good news about family or friends. They always had the potential for new information and updates on peoples' whereabouts.

"*Abuna* John," the boy said, calling me Pastor John. I laughed at his greeting.

"I am not an ordained priest," I said. The boy couldn't believe it. He shook his head in disbelief.

"We were all certain you would be a priest. I thought surely by now you would be. We were counting on you, John."

We talked for some time, asking each other about relatives and our different journeys. When we parted ways, we agreed to visit each other soon. "Next time I see you John, you will be an *abuna*," he said. I laughed kindly and waved goodbye.

As I listened to the familiar sounds of Kakuma that evening, I reflected on the service and the conversation with my relative. His words reminded me that my family had expected me to follow Elijah and carry on his work. It was important for them to know that the next generation would proclaim the message of Jesus. "They counted on me," I thought. I recalled how I once ran through Baping, stopping here and there to pray for people, never knowing for sure what I was doing, but I had blessed them and had been blessed by them. The boy pastor I used to be, the one the village had counted on and looked to, had changed so much over the years. Was this still my calling?

Out of the silence of my soul, Johnson's prophecy came to me, "You will no longer cry, but proclaim this Word." I smiled to myself. Maybe they were all right--Johnson, the villagers, my family, and my pastors. Perhaps one day I would be a priest. Maybe this would be part of my surrendered life.

Now that I was back in the camp, I immersed myself in its spiritual life--learning and working with mentors and pastors and doing the things I loved as a boy, praying with people, teaching and reading God's Word, and preaching the Gospel. I knew that I needed to go forward with my life and applied to the International Organization of Migration to do translation work. I lost myself in the work and took on several shifts. I enjoyed working with people of different backgrounds and cultures. Receiving a small salary, I planned to save this money, hoping to one day see my child. I found that I was able to reconnect with many of the IOM staff who had previously admired my work ethic.

One day, one of the staffers, a young man who helped run the office, began to talk to me about my future. We sat in a hot, overcrowded office with files scattered everywhere. "What would you like to do, John?" he asked.

I had not dreamed much about my future, since my recent sins and failures. I was simply trying to survive in the camp and be faithful to God as best I could. "What do you mean?" I asked.

"Well, what would you most like to do with your life?" the man replied. He sat back in his chair, looking at me, his face open and friendly. Did he really think I could live my dreams and simply do whatever I wanted? I wasn't sure I wanted to think these things again. In the past, they had led me into trouble. I hesitated. I hadn't dared to entertain those thoughts in some time.

"I don't know," I cleared my throat and searched to find the right words. "I have tried many things and failed. I would like to be reunited with my family, my mother, and to see my child. I would like to continue on with my work in the church and I have always longed to receive an education."

The man nodded slowly listening to what I said. "How far are you along in school now?"

"I have managed to get to about a high school level," I told him. He raised his eyebrows in surprise. "I never had the best scores," I said. "I was always in the middle."

He thought for a moment. "I have an idea," he said. "Why don't you apply to take a class at a local Kenyan University? There are many great schools that I am sure would welcome refugees like you. You could use your stipend toward the tuition."

I didn't like the idea of using my savings, but he seemed to think that if we worked together, we might be able to get a partial scholarship, and the cost would be quite small. With my friend's help, I signed up for an intensive course at Daystar University, a Christian undergraduate school in Nairobi.

My friend at the IOM continued to encourage me to work toward receiving an education. He helped me apply for another scholarship to immigrate to Australia. "You will most likely be able to get a theological education there," he said. "There are many seminaries that might accept refugees, especially when they hear of your extensive church work." He was very committed to helping me, and I was so grateful to him that I applied, although I knew I could not leave Kenya without any news of my child.

The time of the class at Daystar approached, but we got the news that there were no partial scholarships, and the cost was more than I could afford. I wondered if this would be another missed opportunity, or if this young man was right. Perhaps God had a plan for me that was greater than my own? "I trust you God," I prayed. "It is your decision." I had surrendered, so I knew that my future was in God's hands, but what I didn't know was that he was working out a plan for me that was better than I dreamed.

It was 2001 and war was still going on in. Due to the recent genocide in Darfur, the international community was slowing taking an interest in Sudan and the persecution that was occurring there.[15] Several South Sudanese refugees had relocated to the United States, and many of them had joined churches. Whole Sudanese communities and churches were formed. Christians in the United States were becoming more interested in the suffering of the Sudanese and were sending missionaries to East Africa.

Tom and Bette Wanous were a missionary couple who had been sent to work at Daystar University. When they visited their son in the United States, they met many South Sudanese refugees who were attending their son's church, and these young men had come from the Kakuma refugee camp. They recounted for them what life was like in the camp. They spoke of the conditions, the disease, starvation, and death. They also spoke of the faith of their

---

15 The Northern government used the oil revenues in the region of Darfur, Sudan to maintain a military occupation. During this occupation in Darfur, the wartime violence affected millions.

peers and their dedication to serving Jesus. They had purchased a few watches to give to their friends back home in Kakuma, and Tom and Bette promised to deliver the watches personally for them since Daystar was a day's trip to Kakuma.

As promised, when Tom and Bette returned to Kenya from their visit to the United States, they traveled to Kakuma Refugee Camp to deliver the watches. They were stunned by the poverty, disease, and starvation. They saw many young, dying children. The suffering was overwhelming. "What can we do?" they asked themselves. "How can we do anything for them?" They prayed for the people in the camp, and their hearts were burdened. They cried out to God and asked, "What can we do?" God told them not to worry, that he, the Lord, would bring the people to them.

The day after their visit to Kakuma, Tom was looking over the class rosters at Daystar University, and he noticed a name which he thought sounded like a Jieng name. He also noticed that the student, John Chol Daau, had never attended the classes for which he had registered. He thought that was odd and inquired about it at the office. He discovered that John was a refugee living at Kakuma and unable to afford the tuition. He talked with Bette that evening and they both wondered if this was part of God's answer to their prayer, "What can we do?" God had brought them the person whom they were called to help!

I had an email account that I had set up through the IOM. I would visit the office from time to time to check the account. On that particular day, I opened my email and saw a message from someone at Daystar, it read, "Dear John, we know that you are a refugee from South Sudan who is currently living at the Kakuma refugee camp and because of the conditions of the camp you are unable to make the tuition to receive an education. We feel called by God to give you a full education and cover the cost of your tuition. We would also be happy to host you while you take classes, but more than that, we would very much like to get to know you. Tell us about yourself. In Christ, Tom and Bette Wanous."

My heart leapt within me. I quickly hit the print key on the computer. I grabbed the printed email and waved it high in the air as if I was awarded a coveted prize. I raced over to my friend's office at the IOM, the one who had tried to help me so many times, and even then, was getting ready to tell me that my scholarship to Australia had fallen through. I held the paper triumphantly, "This is God!" I exclaimed.

My friend, taking the letter from me, read it in disbelief, and relief slowly washed over his face. He embraced me. "I am so happy for you, John. You have worked so hard."

"It is not me. It is God," I said.

Later that evening, I found my pastor, the church leaders, and elders sitting together by the fire, discussing theology. Many of them had built me up in the faith for years.

"I have something I must show you," I stated. "It is from God."

They read the paper together and were amazed. They began to pray and thank God for what he had done. My receiving an education was big news, and the story quickly spread through the camp. I was the most unlikely candidate. They were accustomed to my shy, soft-spoken manner and demeanor. I was not an in-front-of-the-crowd type of leader. I often preferred to stand in the background, happy to serve God quietly. More than that, I wasn't even a priest. I was low in the church order. I hadn't been a pastor for very long, especially when compared with the many other seasoned priests who would have been top choices. I didn't have the experience or the authority of those ahead of me. I didn't have a wife or family, and I had many past sins and struggles. I was an average student, and everyone knew that only the best of the best were able to attend school. Many were surprised by my news, but no one was more surprised than I was.

My lack of merit only confirmed to me that it was God's doing. For several days I carried the email with me and when people stopped me, to question or congratulate me, I took the paper out to show them and said, "This is God." For my whole life, starting from the days when I sat at Elijah's feet to this very moment, I had yearned for an education. It was surreal to think that I was getting the desire of my heart.

When I met with Tom and Bette to discuss my future, we quickly became family. They wanted to hear my story and to help in whatever way they could. They found a small apartment where I could live while I began an associate's degree in community development and Christian leadership. We agreed that I would begin class in 2002, only a year away.

Over the years I had only been able to gather fragments of information about my child. I had learned he was a boy, named Jacob, and that he was healthy. I tried to meet him, writing to him, and sending him little gifts. I wondered if Jacob ever received any of them or if he knew that I wanted to be in his life. I attempted to see him for years, but the family refused to allow me to play any part in his life. I had a small portion of money saved through my work at the IOM. I had saved it for years in the hope that I would one day be able to see him. I took on extensive translation work, including short-term positions with various agencies to earn money for his support. I prayed constantly that I would somehow be allowed to enter into Jacob's life. I simply could not imagine a life never knowing my son. The thought was too terrible.

Through a sudden turn in events, my prayer was answered. Jacob was given the opportunity to spend some extensive time with me, and I would finally be given the chance to know my son. I was overcome with joy and a mixture of emotions. I had lost my father when I was so young, and my only father had been the church. I didn't know if I could be a good father. I longed to be there for Jacob and to bless him. I wanted to give him things I never had. I knew with God's help, all things were possible.

The day came for me to meet Jacob. He stood before me in pressed, western clothing. He appeared small and tentative, with a shy longing on his face. He clutched a small parcel tightly in his hands. How handsome he was! Inexplicable pride, tenderness, and love filled my heart. I knelt beside him and looked into his eyes. I discovered tears were running down my checks. I embraced him freely now, silently calling out to God in gratitude.

As Jacob and I got to know each other, there was transition and difficulty. I was a new father and made mistakes. He had to have the freedom to get to know and trust me. Slowly and over time, we got to know each other and formed a close bond. I took Jacob with me everywhere. He accompanied me to prayer meetings, worship services, and pastoral visits. I remembered how Elijah cared for me and taught me things of the faith, and I wanted to do the same for Jacob. It was an unimagined twist in my life, and I had no way to account for it other than God's generosity to me. I was finally with my son and finally getting an education. This was God.

Chapter Fourteen
WE ARE TO BE SHEPHERDS

When I first stepped off the bus at the Nairobi station, I was confronted by a melee of strange smells, sounds, and sights. I held Jacob's hand a little tighter as we waited for Tom and Bette to pick us up and help us move into our new home. We both had a set of new clothes and one small suitcase between us. We huddled together by the edge of the station, taking in the fast food counters, taxis, the American-style chain restaurants, and all the people. There were people from all over the globe, wearing such clothes as I had never seen before. It was a new world. I looked down at Jacob, his little hand in mine.

"This is new for us, but this is where God wants us, and we can trust him," I said. He nodded and stood a little closer to me. I knew we were both apprehensive. Tom and Bette met us at the station, and together we all drove to what would be Jacob's and my apartment. When we approached the white concrete building, Tom handed me the key. I held it in my hand, turning it over, and laughed out loud. "How does this work?" I asked.

The place was clean and small, but to me, it seemed a small mansion. We had our own beds, something I had never had before. Jacob sat down on one and playfully jumped up and down. I walked around the two rooms, simply taking it all in. In the bathroom I stopped to turn on the sink. Water flowed freely. "Incredible," I whispered, thinking back to my life of drawing water from rivers. I turned the lights off and on. I was just amazed to see them. Living with electricity was another first.

We spent the afternoon learning basic things--where to find the grocery store, how to get to church, and how to find a bus station. We walked to Jacob's new school. He would receive the type of education that I only dreamed of when I was his age. That night as we lay in our beds, the world around us seemed so quiet, so completely still. I could hear only the soft breathing of my son, rather than the chorus of breathing, coughing, and hushed talking one hears when sleeping near thousands of people. And where were the animals calling to each other in the night? Here I could only hear the quiet hum of the fan and the distant sound of traffic. Electric light from the city shown through my window, and outside there was a giant city.

My move to the cosmopolitan city of Nairobi from the Kakuma refugee camp was the greatest cultural shock I had ever experienced. I was a country boy, raised as a shepherd and then a refugee. I was accustomed to a rural, crowded refugee camp with few facilities. I knew nothing about city life, and I experienced a major reorientation. The freedom and anonymity was overwhelming. In the camp, everyone saw my comings and goings. Here in Nairobi, I could take a taxi and go anywhere at any time. The change was quite staggering, and there were many surprises in store for us.

It was my first day of class, and I realized that I stood out in my new suit. Many of my fellow students wore relaxed, stylish western clothing. They carried backpacks and purses. Several of them were younger than I, having just graduated from high school.

"Where are you from, John?" a young Kenyan girl politely asked me.

"I am from South Sudan."

She nodded her head and others chimed in on our conversation, everyone volunteering where they were from, what they hoped to study, where they went to high school, and what their parents did for a living. The majority of them were in their early twenties. They had two parents and brothers and sisters. They had lived the classic life. I knew there were some other orphans at the school, but my story was so different. I had been taken from my parents and forced to run for my life three times. At the lunch table, I found I never quite knew what to share about myself. I often, unwittingly, elicited their concern, sympathy, or confusion.

"Why did you decide to come to Daystar and what do you want to do?" A classmate asked.

The question gave me pause. I didn't decide to come here. It was God who brought Daystar to me, and it was a miracle at that. I have been living in refugee camps for years and never thought I would receive an education. Only one or two out of hundreds are given the chance. God gave me the opportunity, and I must do something good with it to bless his people."

The table was quiet and I knew I had said the wrong thing. I felt that I was on the outside of things, wondering how I could get in. Before this, all I knew was life in the camp where there was little pretense, and we were all in the same situation. Here, however, there was a whole social world and culture that was foreign to me. I didn't know how to dress or talk or act.

Later that afternoon, two classmates asked me more about my history and people. "Why were you forced to run for so many years?" a young man asked.

"Our government was hostile to us, and we couldn't go back. We were young boys. We had no home or place to go. We were just trying to survive."

A young woman nodded her head listening to me. "We are always hearing about the Sudan. Why do you have so many problems? Why can't you solve your problems?" she asked.

Her question wasn't malicious. She sincerely wanted to understand, but how could I explain the suffering and the complex circumstances of my people? How could I account for our sinful and violent history in a way she might understand?

"Many of my people are doing the best they can," I said. "It is a very complex problem. The Northern government wants an Islamist state for all of Sudan. In South Sudan, however, we are indigenous, black people, and we are not Arabs, nor are we Islamic. We are seen as threatening."

That night in my small apartment, after Jacob had gone to sleep, I prayed to God and realized how much I missed my people. How much their burdens were on my heart. I thought of the elderly men and women standing in lines for hours, waiting to get food, when only hours earlier at school a delicious prepared meal had been handed to me on a tray. More than this, I missed our mutual understanding which was shaped through what we had been through, what we had suffered.

"Everything we learn about leadership, development, and even business, starts with Scripture," my professor explained in our first week of class. "The Bible really is the beginning point of our understanding,"

He stood in a crisp suit, in front of a blackboard. A roomful of about thirty students sat in orderly rows around him. I was so impressed with my professor's teaching. I leaned forward in my seat to soak up the things he was saying and listened to the comments of my classmates. We had only begun class fifteen minutes ago, but we were already deep into conversation. I was surprised by how much my peers knew. I was clearly very far behind them, but I had never been a part of such a conversation before, and I wanted to try and understand it all.

Although I had been feeling adrift since my arrival at University, the things I was learning made everything worth it. I simply could not learn enough. I was excited and alive while I was learning. In class I found that my shyness over being a Lost Boy and refugee disappeared. As my professor began to share ideas about leadership and development principles, I found that I had a steady stream of questions. After his lecture concluded, I raised my hand.

"What if you are working with people who have never learned to read or write?" I asked.

My professor nodded, excitedly. "That is a very important question," he said, "often one that is overlooked. Let us begin to address how we might adapt these principles."

The class all joined in the discussion, talking animatedly with their various ideas. I found I was able to share freely and I had practical questions that arose from doing leadership in refugee camps where formal education had never been present and resources were always lacking. After class, I remained to talk with my professor about the lecture.

"I am learning so much from your class," I said.

"John," he said, "your experiences as a refugee help us think about things in a different way. You bring a unique perspective on things, one that many of us have not thought of before. We are happy to have you."

I had never thought of it in those terms. After that day, he would often call on me and ask me to share what my experiences had been in the camp, and what I had seen in my ministry. In time, I realized that I needn't to conform, but could simply be myself. I learned that my background, different as it had been, was also a source of strength.

In those early days, marked by intense learning and study, I began to see something of a miracle, how all the parts of my life, the good and the bad, could be used for God's glory. I knew what it was like to struggle, to be persecuted for following Jesus. I had seen how God can rescue and save desperate people. I knew firsthand how God could meet his people in their pain. This knowledge was a gift and it was something that drew people to me. They wanted to hear what I thought about things, and I knew that I could encourage them because I had been encouraged by Elijah, by my father and mother, by my fellow refugees, and by Jesus who had seen me through it all. I saw that all of us, whether we live in a refugee camp or not, have sorrow and fear, and having had my fair share of things at such a young age, this gave me insight. It allowed me to say to people, "You can get through it. I promise you, Jesus will see you through."

I began to learn what type of leader Jesus was, and the idea of servant leadership changed my life. I had never seen myself as a leader because I was not ordained and preferred to be in the background. I thought leaders were in front with big titles like canon and bishop. A traditional Jieng leader was a chief, a big man in charge, a man with resources, family, and connections. This was the image I had growing up. I had no titles or position, so I did not think of myself as a leader. At Daystar, I learned that a Christian leader simply had to love and serve his people, talking with them, consulting with them, and learning with them. "This is something I can do," I thought to myself one day. "This is something I would love to do."

The things I was learning at Daystar made me reflect on my experiences in the camp. It now seemed that I was living the good life. I had an apartment and three meals a day compared to the one meal ration at Kakuma. More than that, I was learning great things about God and my horizons were broadening.

It was freeing, but even so I missed my church, my friends, my fellow refugees, and my Christian family that I had left behind. They were always on my mind. I could see the elders, the seasoned pastors, men and women who loved and served Jesus for so long, but who had no access to the kind of knowledge I was receiving. This thought nagged at my heart. How might they, too, be transformed? How could they be better leaders? What could I do? I was only one person, and there were thousands of pastors in refugee camps all over East Africa. They needed to learn these precious truths.

When I eventually returned to Kakuma for a visit, my friends were overjoyed to see me. It was amazing to think that after years of struggle, Kakuma was my home and the people there were my family. The overall needs of the camp, its hunger and desperation, were such a contrast to the life I was now living in Nairobi, but still, there was goodness here. We all joined together, drinking tea brewed from strong herbs, sitting in the afternoon shade.

"How have you been, John? Life has been good for you? Tell us all about the new things you have been doing?" an elderly woman in the church asked.

"Oh yes," a young boy jumped in with questions, "what is your apartment like? Have you eaten at Burger King?" They all laughed at his playful humor.

"In my apartment I have running water. I have not yet eaten at Burger King, but I have had hamburgers and spaghetti and all sorts of strange food." I smiled at them, happy to be in their comfortable fellowship once again. I described what the school looked like, what the other students thought, and where they came from. They asked me questions about Nairobi. They were curious to hear all about big city life. They asked me about my education, and a small crowd began to gather around me. For refugees, there is so little entertainment. Visits with long gone friends are always special.

I told them how I was learning about administration, community development, and biblical interpretation. They were hooked. They wanted to hear more. "Tell us more, John. This is very important," they said. "We do not know about these things."

"Well these are just things I have heard," I said. "To be a leader, you have to serve rather than be served." This surprised them. They looked at each other, taken aback.

"How can you do that?" they asked. "As a leader you have to sit and give instructions. People must do what you ask of them. That is how there is order in the church," an elder said and nodded his head with emphasis.

"Christ brings a new order," I replied, "and this order is based on service and sacrifice."

"But, a servant is somebody's slave," they said.

"No," I said. "We are only slaves to Christ, but out of love for him, we follow the model of obedience he gave us. It was that way when Jesus washed the disciples' feet. He was showing us what servant leadership was like."

This made them fall silent. There were twenty different furrowed faces, thinking intently. "Tell us more, John," someone said.

"I don't know what else to tell you," I said. "I have told you all about my classes."

"Just say anything. Say whatever comes to your mind. Just open your mouth and talk," a church mother instructed me.

Not wanting to let her down, I began to talk about a lecture I remembered that modeled Christian leadership taken from the life of Joseph in the Old Testament. As I talked, I thought of what to say next. What else had I learned that they might want to know? A memory popped into my mind or something a professor or classmate had said, and I shared it with them. Having been deprived of education for so long, they craved knowledge. They desperately wanted to learn more, and they didn't seem to mind that that it came out in a jumble. I talked until late that evening, simply trying to remember the things I had learned. I felt embarrassed to have so many leaders listening to me, but they goaded me on.

"We must stop here," I said. "I have talked for too long," I said, sincerely.

"No, John, you have learned so much, we want to hear more."

Shyly I began to describe a paper topic on business management. It occurred to me as I was rambling on that these leaders had been pastors for several years. They were self-taught and possessed a wealth of knowledge, but had never experienced a formal theological education. There were realities and ideas they never had the opportunity to explore. They saw instantly that the knowledge I was gaining would be invaluable to them and could fortify and strengthen their ministries. They had a deep desire to learn more. Their situation was quite different from the typical westerner who is so inundated with information and ideas that the importance of true knowledge can be easily overlooked or forgotten. Here, with my people, information was one of the most valuable commodities available. New ideas did not often circulate through the refugee camp, but when they did, they were precious.

On the bus back to Nairobi, I looked out the window, watching the country slowly roll into the city. Lost in my thoughts, I felt a stirring in my soul. I knew something significant had occurred, but I didn't know what to make of it. I wished I could do something for my friends. Once again, I felt the old angry burn from the injustice of refugee life. It was wrong that these leaders could not receive the education for which they were starved. My thoughts were riddled with doubt. I knew I had to do something, but what? I was not qualified to teach, and even if I could teach the pastors, how could I go about it? Their context and experiences, the war, the refugee camp, the trek, made them such a unique group of people. Many of them had never learned English, or learned to read or write. I didn't see how formal universities or seminaries could reach them.

That evening, back in my Nairobi flat, I got down on my knees and prayed a simple prayer. "Lord Jesus," I began, "you have showed me something today, that your people are hungry for knowledge. Show me what to do and how to do it."

After the prayer, I knelt in silence and pictures from my days in the cattle camps came back to me. I remembered running after my cows, cleaning them, and calling to them. I felt a strong longing to return there. I remembered certain boys with whom I played and worked and the fun we had among our cattle. I recalled the various cows I looked after. Each cow had been different, a different appearance, a different personality. I had always respected my cattle. The elders of the camp stood out in my mind. There was a dignity and pride in their position. They understood, to an impressive degree, all the varied components of their work and livelihood. The cattle camp had a spirit, a philosophy, and a way of life. It was a part of who I was, and it was integral to my people. It was something that the Jieng in the refugee camp missed so much.

"What are you showing me?" I whispered to the Father. "Do you want me to return to the cattle camp? After all this, am I to be a shepherd?" I was mystified as to what God wanted for me. That night I went to bed more confused than ever.

Over the next several days, my mind kept wandering back to the camp and my old life among the cattle. "Why do I keep thinking of my cows?" I thought. I suspected that the Lord was trying to tell me something, but I wasn't sure what. Questions were at the center of my prayers and thoughts, until one day, in deep confusion, I knelt before God again. Praying, I felt a strong presence beside me, and a stillness came over me. I held my breath, and then I heard God speak, "I am the Good Shepherd." Something connected in my spirit, and I knew what Jesus was telling me. I found my Bible and turned to one of my favorite passages from John's gospel.

> I am the good Shepherd; I know my sheep and my sheep know me – just as the Father knows me and I know the Father – and I lay down my life for the sheep. I have other sheep that are not of this sheep pen. I must bring them also. They too will listen to my voice, and there shall be one flock and one Shepherd. (John 10:14-16)

"I am to be a shepherd," I thought, "but of a different kind!" I finally understood. Jesus was bringing me back to the cattle camp, because this was the way the refugee leaders could understand who God was and how they could serve him. My visions were not a message to return to the cattle camp, but rather, they revealed that Jesus was the ultimate shepherd. Their life at the cattle camp had prepared the pastors to be shepherds. This is the way I can teach them, I realized. This is how they will understand.

When I visited the camp again, I felt a sense of clear direction. I was no longer confused or bitter by the injustice of refugee life. I knew that God was speaking to me and to my people, and that changed everything. The church leaders organized a time for me to teach, and about thirty priests, deacons, and lay leaders attended. Under the great big trees, in the afternoon shade, we gathered. This time I didn't feel so embarrassed, but I simply began to describe what God had shown me.

"I want to begin with the topic of servant leadership," I said. "How are we to be leaders? How are we to teach people and shepherd them in the faith?" The crowed was quiet as they thought over the question. "Do you remember the cattle camps?" I asked. They all murmured and nodded, that yes, they remembered. How could they forget? It had been their livelihood for so long. "What was the instruction our elders taught us in the camp?" I asked.

"You need to know your cattle," said one man. "You have to be able to distinguish them from all the rest."

"Right," I said. "You must know their color and shape. You must know each cow by name, and the cows responded to you did they not?" There was laughter in the room, for all of them remembered how certain cows came to know and respond to their owners without error. The cattle demonstrated affection for their shepherd. There were even bulls who were instructed to sing a type of basic song to their masters. These beasts mimicked our calls.

"Yes," said an elderly man. "The cows always responded to my song,"

The leaders in the cattle camps invented a song that only their cows would know. The leaders would sing their songs to their cows as a way to gather them. It was a way to keep their herd together and not lose any cows.

"And, what would we do if we lost a single cow?" I asked.

"We would run for hours, sometimes days, to find it." They replied, nearly in unison. The excitement in the room grew as we visited a topic we loved and knew so well.

"And what would we do if a cow was sick or weak or in danger?"

"You had to sacrifice yourself," someone said. He stood passionately with raised hands in the air, "You would sleep with your cow, providing constant care. You had to risk your own life for your cattle, because they were your cattle!"

"Yes," I said. "That is all true. That was our way of life in the cattle camp. It was the only way we knew. There are many of us who, being refugees, thought our training in the camps was lost forever, that we would never get to return to our cattle camp life, but don't you see that God was training us all this time to be leaders in his church? We are to be shepherds as he was the Good Shepherd. In John's Gospel, Jesus tells us, what kind of leader he is and how we are to be leaders too, and it is very similar to the things we learned in the cattle camp, but it is much bigger than the camp, because it involves the world and all God's people. We were taught to sacrifice for our cattle, to protect them from all injury and disease, to strengthen them, and to go to great lengths for just one of them. This is how we are to be leaders in God's church. We are to be shepherds."

The group was extremely animated and energized by these words. They took turns standing up, sharing their thoughts and responses to the teaching. It spoke to their lives and their experiences. They opened the Bible and read through John chapter ten. They took turns sharing stories from the cattle camp and the training they had received there. They shared the things that they had learned as priests, deacons, and lay leaders. They made connections between the two worlds, and they saw for the first time how they related to each other. They saw their ministries in a new way, and it was as if God's Word, written so long ago, was tailored just for them. I was amazed to see how God used their experiences and history to speak to them, in the perfect way. A way that only they could understand. He showed them a vision for how they could live and flourish, and he spoke in a way that was unique to them. God was not far away, he was close.

Deeply moved by my time of teaching at Kakuma, I made arrangements to come again during my next school break. When I returned, I stayed longer and met with a wide variety of people, not just the elders in the faith. Several young people also came to hear my teaching. This time, I was able to bring a professor with me from Daystar. He had volunteered to teach a short-term class. It was wonderful to see how the people responded to my professor's teaching. I began to organize more classes in Kakuma, and they grew in popularity. The word spread, and persons from other camps asked me to come and teach them as well.

There were over 2,000 pastors in the Kakuma refugee camp alone, the vast majority of whom had little theological training. Through my connections at Daystar, I was able to bring in gifted and highly qualified teachers and professors to help teach short-term classes. I came to see that this was not simply a side project. I knew that God was calling me to dedicate my life to this work. He gave me a vision to start a seminary, a school for refugees and for his people. I called it Good Shepherd Leadership Training Institute. Within the first year we reached over 1,000 refugees, and the people continued to come.

The situation in my homeland was still volatile and required Christians who were equipped to be peacemakers and leaders. The war had torn our country apart. I knew if one day I could return to South Sudan I would help rebuild what had been lost. All the years prepared me to train others. Years of wandering and questioning came to an end. This was my calling - the purpose of my life.

Chapter Fifteen
GOD IS YOUR MOTHER

I arrived at the dusty refugee camp along the Sudanese and Ugandan border. I was tired and thirsty from days of traveling, but nothing could stop me from this reunion. There were so many years between us, and now I was a grown man. She would be much older, an old woman, but she was my mother and my family. I had worn my best suit, which was now wrinkled and dusty from my journey. I smoothed out the crinkles and adjusted my knapsack and Bible.

I made my way through the camp. Groups of people sat outside their *tukuls* chatting. Boys played a lively game of soccer. I felt growing excitement in my heart and something I couldn't name or express. Some intangible sadness of years passed and of course, I was nervous. It had been thirteen years since I had been with my family and I had tried my best, like all other refugees, to put our story together. Having no word of Mother in years, a part of me had resigned myself to her death.

She wouldn't know that I was coming; there had been no way to contact her. I planned out what I would say to her when I saw her. I wanted to make her feel at ease. I saw a group of young people, around my own age, talking and laughing together. I approached a young girl sitting a little outside the circle.

"Excuse me sister, do you have a glass of water?" She sprang to her feet and came back with what looked like a small bowl. I took a small sip, not wanting to presume on her generosity, and handed it back to her.

"Take more," she said laughing.

I must have looked thirsty. I paused to enjoy the cool taste on my tongue and sighed deeply. I mustered up the courage to ask her about Tabitha Daau. I knew that even though she was listed on the camp register, she might not be there. The only way to know was to search among the people who truly knew the inside and outs of the camp. There was still a chance I might not find her and this entire trip had been in vain.

"Do you know Tabitha Daau?" I asked the young woman and handed her back the bowl.

"Oh yes," her face lit up. "She is one of our mothers. She lives close by." She pointed in the direction of where I could find her.

I realized that I had been praying silently. "Thank you Jesus," my spirit cried inside me.

The girl was staring at me, wondering who I was, and then, it dawned on her. "You are her son!" she said, beaming and embraced me as if I were her long lost brother.

"She must love Mother," I thought, "to be so happy for her."

"She always talks of you. Oh, thank God you are here!"

She brought me over to the others in the little group, and they became excited, hugging and congratulating me.

"We will walk you to her," she said, pulling my sleeve before I could answer. Sensing my nervousness, they began gently leading me along.

"Tabitha, Tabitha," they said, nearly squealing, "God has blessed you today."

They playfully pulled at me, so that I would hurry along. The joy of reunion was contagious, and I was thankful to be helped in such a time. My heart was racing, about to explode in my chest, and my thoughts weren't clear. We walked past many *tukuls,* and the girls talked and laughed the whole time. They stopped abruptly and pointed.

"There she is," they said, pushing me forward. I recognized her instantly and once again, I was a young boy racing home from the cattle camps to see Mother waiting for me by the hearth. She was sitting outside her *tukul* enjoying the sunshine.

I was looking into a dream coming to life. I could only stand there and stare. She was the same, only older and slightly wearier, but her strength was striking. It must have developed over years of fight to stay alive. I could only imagine what she had been through, and it grieved me deeply. She had been on her own for years. She must have thought I was dead. Filled with tenderness for her, tears came. I wiped them away on my sleeve. It was then she looked up from her bench. She gasped loudly, clasping her hands together. She made a sound, something between a laugh and a cry. Jumping to her feet, she began running toward me, smiling and laughing all at once. Somewhere behind me, I could hear the girls cheering.

"Mother," I said, embracing her.

"My son," she said. Trembling slightly, she griped my arms. She looked down at her feet, unable to find the right words to say. For a moment, I worried for her, she was shaking all over.

"Chol Makeyn. My son, my firstborn son," she touched my face as if trying to prove I was real and not a dream, but I knew the dream was coming to life.

I held her hands firmly to steady her and led her over to the shade. We sat down under the trees on a bench. She looked at me with happiness and disbelief, taking in my face after all this time. Her eyes were alight and intense, filled with tears. At once, I could tell she had something she wanted to share with me. A great burden was on her heart. People came out of their *tukuls* to see what the commotion was. They were smiling and waving to us, yelling congratulations. We looked at each other for a long time, taking in what God had done. I didn't quite know what to say to her. I wanted to say something to make her comfortable, but no words came. The speech I had rehearsed was forgotten. She wore an old dress which must have been given to her. She still had her hands clasped, resting in her lap. She was filled, nearly brimming over with unspoken emotion. So much joy, but I could tell sadness, too. Finally, she broke the silence.

"Have you still followed Elijah's God?" she asked. She looked at me, searching my face.

"Yes, I have," I said. "I have been following Jesus Christ all this time."

She uttered a great sigh of relief and her shoulders fell. More tears came to her eyes. It was as if a great weight had been taken from her, and she began to weep freely, her shoulders shuddering. I put my arm around her and let her cry.

"Oh, I am glad, John. I am so glad. I thought I would never get to be your mother again, but I knew that God could be a mother for you. I knew that God could do better than I ever could do. So I trusted him all these years to be your mother for you. I prayed for you every day that God would come and be the mother I couldn't be, and today after all these years, I now know that he has heard my cry." Her hands shook as she spoke, and I lightly squeezed her hand to reassure her.

"He has been a mother and father to me, Mother. Don't worry. My church has been my family, but I have missed you."

"I have missed you, too, my son. My son returned to me today." She patted me and all the maternal affection of years was in her touch. Tears rolled down her cheeks. "I am praising God," she said.

I told her what camps I had been in and how we had been forced to flee three times. I described what life had been like in the camps, how I had been a group leader and had became a pastor. I told her about my son, Jacob, what he was like, and how she must meet him. I told her how I had searched for her in Mogali for months, but never found her. I described to her the miraculous way God had given me an education and allowed me to share it with others.

"God has answered my prayer and given you so much more than I ever thought," she said.

The conversation flowed naturally now, and joy was overcoming the sadness, but I knew that there was more to get through, painful questions to answer. We sat in her *tukul*. She had very little to offer, which I could tell was troubling her, but she made a stew out what little ingredients she had. I suggested we take a walk and that she show me around the camp. As we walked, there were many introductions, laughter, and congratulations. Our reunion was an encouragement to all.

"Why don't you show me where you worship?" I asked. She led me to their outdoor church whose benches, made from tree branches, were arranged in a semi-circle. We sat on one as the sun began to sink in the west. It wasn't as hot and crowded as Kakuma. There was a pleasant breeze, and I felt the peace of something from my home and family being restored to me.

"What has it been like for you, Mother? Where have you been?"

She told me her story. There was a part of me that didn't want to know, because it would be painful, but I knew I had to hear. On the day of the invasion, she saw Father die from gunshots. She wanted to do something for him, but she was forced to flee because men were pointing guns at her head. She fled to the forest with the others. She looked for Joseph and me there. She called to Joseph and me, frantically asking after us.

"I hoped you were not dead," she said. "I ran and I looked for you. I did not make it to the border, but I hid in the forest with the others. I wanted to stay there because I felt too weak to go on, and the others who were with me left me there. I had to run and hide alone. The enemy nearly found me many times before I made it to a camp. It was a horrible place in the beginning. There were so many of us, and we were all lost and hurt. All the men were gone. There were so many children without mothers, and I had lost my sons. I can't describe what it was like to lose my sons. It was as if I was torn in two, and the other half was gone. There were many times I wanted to die, but I told myself that you were still alive and one day, I would find you. I prayed to Elijah's God every day and asked him to give me strength. One day, he lifted up my head and told me to look around. I saw motherless children crying out in need, and I told myself that I could be a mother to these young children. They put fifty-six of us together in a large hut. They were all young girls, ages ten to seventeen, and I became their mother. They were heartbroken, and there was no one to care for them, and I had lost my sons to care for. We were often very afraid, and I would sleep by the door to ease their fear. I'd say to them, 'Sleep well and don't worry. I am at the door. If anything comes, it will start with me.'"

"They often cried and asked me, 'Where is my father, where is my mother?' I never knew what to tell them, but I tried to give them hope. I would pray for them and say, 'God, they don't know where their mother or father is. I don't know where my sons are, but I know, God, one day we will meet them again.'"

She had been strong and courageous all these years. I wondered how her faith had grown so strong over the years and how she knew so much about God. She had been a Christian for only one year when our village was invaded.

She was weeping now, letting out years of pent-up sadness. She clasped my hand. "I have not taught you," she said. "There is nothing of me for you to remember. I have not lived with you or been there for you. I have not done for you what I would have as your mother, but I know God is doing it for you. He is parenting and teaching you. I have nothing more to tell you than what God has already told you, so keep on with God."

She wept for some time, and then drew a deep breath. We began to put more lost pieces together, where we had been and what information we had of friends and relatives. Joseph, I discovered, was alive. I would see my little brother again, and my heart swelled at the thought. We talked until late in the afternoon, and then we went to her *tukul* to have dinner together with many Christian friends who were so happy for Tabitha.

I stayed with my mother for two weeks. It took me a while to get accustomed to the idea that she really was my mother, and that she was very much alive. I met many new friends, heard stories, and worshiped with her neighbors. Mother carried her Bible with her everywhere she went, despite the fact that she had never learned to read. She knew the book was sacred, and she understood its contents. I playfully quizzed her over Bible stories to see what she actually knew, but she answered all my questions correctly.

The evening before I left to return to my studies, three girls joined Mother and me for dinner. They were with Mother at the first refugee camp and had managed to remain together these past fourteen years. They were part of the fifty-six she cared for. We sat together in the open air around the fire and ate beans and fried dough the girls had brought. They told many stories of how Mother had protected them, and how she slept at the door to keep them safe, praying for them and nurturing them through the years.

"Brother," the eldest girl said, "Tabitha has been a wonderful mother to the three of us. She never quit talking of her dear sons and how we would meet them one day and now we have." She glowed in the firelight and patted Mother lightly on the hand. I could see the love she felt for her.

"We have learned so much from your mother," one of the girls told me. "She always said, 'My son is somewhere. I don't know where, but God is taking care of him. One day you will meet him. He is your brother.'"

Hearing these stories I was overwhelmed by the scope of Mother's sorrow, that she had lived so long with the painful distance between us, and by her faith. She never gave up hope that God would redeem our family's struggles and bring us together again.

"We have lost all our brothers," one of the girls said. "We always wanted a brother and your mother told us that we could have you once she got you back."

We all laughed together. We had all lost our families, and so we learned how God was making a new family, and that he could do it in all times and places. As the girls began to leave for the evening we prayed.

"Jesus Christ, thank you for my sisters and thank you for our mother. We thank you that you have given us a family in you. That we are not orphans, but mothers, sons, brothers, and sisters." We said "Amen" in unison.

Mother and I watched them as they walked away in the dark, starlit night, and I felt a shared spirit with them. What Mother had promised so long ago was true. We were brothers and sisters.

People came and went, talking around the fire as the evening unfolded. Mother was wrapped in an old shawl, and we watched the fire grow dim. We felt comfortable sitting in silence, enjoying the blessings God had given, but there was one last question.

"Mother," I said at last, "father is dead and Joseph is alive, but what of Elijah? Is he alive?"

She hung her head and closed her eyes, as if in pain. I knew at once. "No son, Elijah died several years ago."

The sadness took hold, as I knew it would. I owed my faith to my uncle, the faith that had saved and sustained us through it all. I wanted to talk to him one last time. I wanted to say, "Thank you." As a boy, I never realized what I had been given, but over the course of my life, I had learned that he had given me the very life of Christ.

"Do we know how?" I asked. She shook her head. I hated not knowing. I had lived never having the answers I needed. I instinctively knew that I had to go visit my uncle's people, to honor his memory and to learn what happened to him, to Baping, and to see what, if anything remained. I would return to Southern Sudan. I would travel along the villages and see the shepherd boys run along the river with their flocks. I would drink fresh milk from a gourd and turn my eyes to skies that I had known as a boy.

"Prayer Synagogue" in Nimule, Southern Sudan, 2006

Homecoming after seventeen - year absence due to civil war

Participants of Good Shepherd College and Seminary 2015

Rev. John Chol Daau, Bishop Abraham Nhial, and Rev. Samuel Marial Nyumanzi Refugee Camp, 2015

Good Shepherd Theological Training Institute Avilo 11 Refugee Camp, 2015

Chapter Sixteen

CHASING AFTER THE CROSS

The scenes were familiar--the earth, the sky, the rivers. Much of the beauty I remembered had remained, and yet, it was a changed land. It was poorer, nearly all the infrastructure, schools and clinics, were wiped out due to the destruction of war. The signs of it were everywhere. In 2005, North and South Sudan signed the Comprehensive Peace Agreement, making it safe for the first time in nearly twenty years for refugees to return to South Sudan. After seventeen years, I finally returned home. I was brought back to my life under the trees, the cattle camps, and the way I used to beat the drum while the shrines burned to the ground. I could almost hear our singing in the wind and see our fires swirling in the late afternoon skies. I remembered how the name of Jesus swept through the village, stronger than any famine or war, and I knew that after all these years his name had endured. His presence was with us as strong as ever.

I traveled to Baping by foot. Children came out of their *tukuls* to greet me, as visitors were rare in these parts. The remains of the village were still to be found. Most of the *tukuls* had been lost, but some of the people were still there, and there were many reunions with those who remembered me. "Madioor," they called to me, "we remember you!" Men and women stopped what they were doing, throwing down their work to greet me. I stopped and talked with people from my childhood, recalling our history together.

"Do you remember how we learned of Elijah's God together and the amazing teaching he brought to us?" one of them asked.

"Of course I do," I said, happy to hear that Elijah's teaching was remembered. How could I have forgotten it? My entire life, in many ways, was built upon his teaching.

"I remember you," a lady neighbor said, "and how you would beat your drum and dance."

Her laughter bubbled up, and I felt myself a shy boy again. It was good to see them and hear their stories. I discovered what friends had survived and who was gone. I learned what had happened to them. I ate with them, and we took shade together under the tamarind trees.

While touring the villages, I asked about my family members. I was told that my uncle, Johnson, the one who quieted me as an infant and brought me to church, was still alive and living in the next village. This was the first sign of any living relative in the area, and I knew at once I had to see him. A group of people agreed to walk with me, taking me to him.

It had been years since I had seen him, but immediately I knew he was of my clan. He was now a much older man and living humbly. He sat in a chair outside his *tukul,* enjoying the afternoon breeze. I thought back to thirty years ago when he was a man my age, the words that he proclaimed over me, and the book he had given me. Had his words and that one moment forever changed the path of my life? He smiled when he saw me, his face a mass of wrinkles and light.

"I remember you," he said, rising slowly from his chair. "You used to cry a lot, but I held the Bible over your eyes." With shaky hands, he took my hand in his. Years of warfare had taken a toll on his body, and he was slightly bent, but his spirit was strong. He was pleased to learn that I had remained a Christian and a leader in the faith.

"Tell me, *Chol Makeyn*, did you talk a lot about God's Word?"

"Yes, I believe I have. It has seen me through many things."

"You have followed Jesus all this time?" he asked. His eyes were bright, almost mischievous.

"Yes, Uncle, all this time, I have never forgotten him."

His face was filled with wonder to have me at his doorstep after so many years. I, too, in that moment, was mesmerized by the passage of time between us and our connecting in this way once again.

"Then it is true what Elijah and I thought about you," he said. He leaned back in his chair satisfied. "Today I know that it is true. You have been a true compensator, as was prophesied years ago, when I held the Bible over your eyes and commanded you to tell its story." I smiled, humbled by his words.

Johnson began to tell me his story of many years and how he had started his church. He had lived his life for God, and always took his Bible with him. "I knew that I was blessed to have a Bible," he said, "few of us had one." Before the war broke out, he left the city and the factories to escape the religious persecution, threats, and ever-increasing violence. He did not travel to Baping, the way his cousin Elijah had, but had gone to the neighboring village. When he walked into the town, he was carrying his precious Bible. The people thought it was strange. They had never seen such a book.

"Hey, Johnson, what are you carrying?" they asked him.

"I am carrying my Bible, my sacred book, about the God of heaven."

It was embarrassing when they laughed at him, but Johnson persisted in telling them more about the Bible. He explained how the God of heaven and earth, Jesus Christ, was the Savior of the world. Johnson walked to the fish camp where many of the men congregated to catch fish together. There was a man, a *tiet* of the traditional African religion, who was known for multiplying the number of fish. Every evening this man would bring in a large catch, and from what he divined in the fish, he would tell people their fortunes.

"You have a spell on your life," the *tiet* would say. "You must be careful or you will die." He put fear in their hearts. They gathered around him to hear his predictions. When the *tiet* saw Johnson enter the fish camp, he was afraid. Running in fear, he crouched behind a bush. It wasn't just Johnson that frightened him, but there was something about Johnson's Bible that caused him to recoil and leap back. Hysteria visibly grew in him.

"Get that young boy away!" he shrieked. Johnson, reaching out his arms in peace, moved forward to speak to the *tiet*, but the old man shrank back and shuddered. He muttered to himself and began to run about in a fitful circle. He threw his arms in the air wildly and shouted, "Don't let him come near me!"

The people stood by, amazed. The *tiet* was afraid of this man. How could the *tiet* be afraid? He was to be feared. He was the one with power and authority.

Taking several steps back, Johnson calmly looked at the *tiet* from a distance, attempting to show him he meant no harm. The *tiet* relaxed a little. No longer shaking, he stood still and stared at Johnson in radiating hostility, as if challenging him to a fight. Johnson didn't know what to do.

Quite Suddenly, the *tiet* looked at Johnson, and covered his eyes. He pointed to his Bible, "Your book is burning my eyes! What you have is powerful on me." He sat down on the ground, as if he physically weak, and crossed his legs. He would not let Johnson move closer to him.

Johnson was unsure of his next move. His heart was filled with compassion for the man, but Johnson was also determined to show that what the *tiet* represented was wrong. At that moment, the Spirit spoke to Johnson and inspired within him a song. In a loud clear voice, he began to sing to the *tiet*. It was the best way to communicate with him. He knew the song would reach him.

> The power of the Father is in the hand of Jesus.
> Where will you surrender, if you won't believe in Jesus?
> He is the Way, the Truth, and the Life eternal.
>
> The chief magician saw me holding the Bible.
> He shouts, "Eei, eei my eye.
> Where is this person coming from, the person who took my power away?"
> Don't take it for granted, the taking of the blessed food,
> And the Blood poured for us.
>
> The Great Shepherd is searching for his Father's sheep.
> He will tie them to the *löc*.[16]
> For love he loved us,
> And he guarded us, saved us and all of us.
>
> You will be filled with the Father's power.
> You will be filled with the Father's power.
> He saves us and he has tenderness for us.
>
> You will find him and don't reject him.
> You will find him and don't reject him.
> In the name of the Father, the Son,
> and the Holy Spirit, Amen.[17]

---

16 This is a thick piece of wood hammered down on solid ground (mostly with clay soil) to tie down a cow or any other domestic animal.

17 "Hold, Hold Your Child," was written by Johnson Deng Awuok in the late 1970s and is a popular Jieng Hymn. Translation by Rev. Samuel Galuak Marial, March 2011.

"What I have is of life," Johnson said. "It is not trying to hurt you. You need to believe in the name of the Father, Son, and Holy Spirit."

The *tiet* remained sitting on the ground and considered his words. Johnson moved closer to him and opened his sacred book and began to explain the great story contained within in it. The *tiet* listened for a long time, thinking and considering. After hours of listening and thinking, he said, "I believe."

When the *tiet* turned to Jesus, the people knew that Johnson's book was true. How else could his eyes have burned? Why would the *tiet* give up his spiritual power and authority if it were not true? Johnson's Bible and the *jok* or Spirit it revealed must be real. It was that Great *Jok*, the true God that was more powerful than all the gods whom they worshiped and to whom they had offered sacrifices. Johnson's Bible had conquered the *tiet*! It revealed the truth and it spoke of miracles much greater than telling fortunes and multiplying fish. It told of a God and man, Jesus, who was raised from death to life, the one who broke all curses! It promised that they too would be raised from death to life. It spoke of salvation from death, healings, and deliverances. It was stronger and better than the *tiet*, and it was true!

They named the church the *Jok* of Johnson's Bible. They chose that name because, at that time, they knew only of the great drama between the God of Johnson's Bible and the *tiet*. The God of Johnson's Bible became their God and they established their church for him alone.

Johnson Awouk Deng told of the spiritual battle between his God and the *tiet* in a song, the same song he was inspired to sing when he saw this man. The song is sung in Jieng churches to this day. I grew up singing this song and now learned it was from him.

"Uncle, have you ever written another song?" I asked him. He shook his head no.

"I never wrote another song, but I still have my Bible."

This was the Bible that burned the *tiet's* eyes and opened mine. It was the Bible that held the great story, the story he commissioned me always to tell. He showed me its weathered pages, and it was still his prize. It was wonderful to reunite with Johnson, but I still had questions about the death of my uncle, Elijah. Those questions burned in my heart from the moment I saw Johnson.

"If you travel to the next village," Johnson said, "you can meet with his wife, Tabitha. She has recently returned from camp and is alive and well. She will tell you what you need to know."

That evening, I stayed and ate with Uncle Johnson. We told many old stories and put the pieces of our family life together. He could not make the trip to the neighboring village with me, but sent a few of our clan members to accompany me along the way.

From boyhood, I had known Tabitha. She had a powerful ministry of taking care of people. She was still a Christian and still had her ministry. She took care of many people, some of her own children as well as those who were orphaned by the war. She was in her sixties, but her *tukul* was filled with children. She was a mother to them all.

"*Chol Makeyn*," she said, drawing me close. Her eyes were shining, wet with tears. "How I wish your uncle could see you. Oh, how happy he would be to see his *Chol Makeyn*." I sat down cross-legged on her mat and accepted a cup of tea.

"I have so many questions for you, auntie." She nodded her head in understanding. She knew I needed to hear the story of my uncle.

"We all miss Elijah. He was so strong for all of us," she said.

"How did Elijah die?" I asked. "Was he killed by soldiers?"

She shook her head. "No, Elijah lived for many more years and continued to do church work. We always prayed for you,

Chol Makeyn, that you were alive and that Jesus would continue to strengthen you."

I looked down at my tea cup, listening to her words. I was thankful to know that he always cared for me, always prayed for me through the years.

"Have you continued with your Uncle's work, as he always hoped you would?" she said. Her face was clear and earnest. I knew this meant a great deal to them. They had been counting on me to proclaim the Word.

"Yes, I have. I have never forgotten the things he taught me. That teaching has seen me through so many things. When we were forced to run, I knew only of Uncle Paul's healing and how Jesus was able to do what no other *tiet* could. In time, I have learned so much more of his strength and power. He has brought me to this place, and I can never forget him."

"That is right!" she said, her eyes glistened with tears as she remembered all that happened in our small village. "God was so good to us in those days. He met us when we needed him, but I have not answered your question, *Chol Makeyn*," she said and squeezed my hand in her motherly fashion. She took a deep breath, and I could tell that the story of Uncle's passing was painful even after all these years.

"Elijah didn't die during the invasion, but it did break his heart as it did to all of us, but he lived on for years. The war seemed to only drive him forward, and the people needed to hear his testimony and teaching more than ever. His words gave so many of us hope. Funerals and baptisms, he preached at them all. He worked tirelessly until he became ill. He always had pain in his stomach, but we were so trapped here, and there was no hospital, so all we could do was pray and hope that one day the pain would go away. He carried on for some time, always preaching, always teaching. He eventually died from appendicitis."

I was shocked. Appendicitis was a common illness, one that could have been easily treated if there had been access to medical ies, but because of the war, no medical attention was available. He had died needlessly. Tabitha was crying now as she continued to tell the story.

"We carried him on blankets for nearly eighteen hours to receive medical help. We got very close," she said softly. "He died on the road to the clinic." Her words were a mere whisper. She smoothed away the tears and attempted a smile. "Come," she said to me, rising from her mat, "We can visit his grave."

We walked to a cool, shaded part of the village and found ourselves in a little clearing. There was no name on the grave. It was marked by a single cross. I knelt beside his grave, lost in thoughts of him. I saw my uncle's face as he described to me my namesake, John the Baptist, and I heard the passion in his voice as he taught me the song about the wild man in the desert. I remembered how he patiently answered my questions. His unwavering faith and a deep love for was a strong pillar. He had given that to me, and I was thankful. The time I had been with him was short, but it changed me forever.

"Did he want to tell me anything before he died?" I asked.

She shook her head no. "All he said was 'take care of the churches of God,'" she said. "He said that over and over. At his death bed, he called me over to him, and there were a few of his fellow pastors there as well. We gathered around him and listened carefully to his instructions, but he only had one, 'Take care of God's people and make sure you spread the Gospel. Keep doing the work God has given you. I am now going. We will meet again. Take care of the churches of God.'"

Faithful to the end, I thought. Throughout his life, Elijah had possessed a singular focus to which he dedicated his life. In his short lifetime, he had planted nearly forty churches. He never valued clan, tribe, ancestry, or possessions ahead of the Gospel. Most Jieng men at their death bed take the time to bequeath their livestock and possessions to the next generation. It is the moment they make their will and last wishes known. Elijah had only one wish and ultimately only one possession. Elijah handed what he most treasured, God's Word, to the next generation.

"If he were here," I asked, "what do you think he would say to me?"

"I think," Tabitha said, "he would not say anything apart from 'take care of the churches of God.' Don't follow the advice of this world. You must follow in his footsteps. You must continue to preach this Word. Even if he were here, there is nothing he could give you except this Word, so you must continue this path."

Her words echoed the same prophesy that Johnson had prayed over me as a baby. "From this time on, you will no longer cry, but proclaim this Word." I felt that I had been brought back to the beginning, that I was now grasping something that had been promised long ago.

As I stood by the grave, I saw the sun setting over the village and stretching out to all the villages of the Jieng people. It was a ball of fire in the afternoon sky, its light reflected by the brilliant, green trees. Hushed voices, music, the smell of ashes, my uncle's face, men and women long gone, seemed to be all around me, and in the center, stood a single cross over an unmarked grave. It could have belonged to any one of us - the many brothers and sisters in the faith who died with the Gospel on their lips.

Wrapped gently in the golden sunlight, I listened to the branches swaying in the breeze, and I thought back to all the years that had brought me to this place. Life had been touched by so much tragedy. I lost my father and uncle and there were so many others who were gone. I thought of the friends I buried, the elderly left behind in the forest to die, the girls lost to slavery, and the young boys who dried up and shattered like glass. I thought back to the struggles of refugee life, the humiliation of the food lines, the hunger, and disease. I reflected on my own sins. I had found Jesus in the midst of it all, always there, like the cross we placed among the ashes of the burned shrines. There was glory rising in the tragedy. God had been kind to us. He had been given us the most valuable thing of all, the Word Himself, Jesus Christ, who had been with me since infancy. I saw that now. I was standing on the teaching of my ancestors, on the foundation of my Great Ancestor, Jesus Christ. My whole life I had not simply been running through thorns, from one tragedy to the next, but to someone, the Redeemer of all. I had been chasing after the cross of Christ. Years of running had brought me to this final truth--Jesus was the endpoint and the beginning. *From this time on, you will no longer cry, but proclaim this Word.*

EPILOGUE

It is estimated that over two million people died in the Second Civil War of Sudan and over four million Southern Sudanese people were displaced. Of the estimated 30,000 Lost Boys, only 10,000 survived the journey. Some were as young as four years old. In 2005, the war between North and South Sudan legally ended with the signing of the Comprehensive Peace Agreement between the Northern Government and the Sudanese Peoples' Liberation Army. In recent years, the situation in Southern Sudan has changed dramatically. On January 9, 2011, there was a referendum for Southern succession from the Northern government. Of the 3.8 million registered voters, the referendum was passed with 98.83 percent in favor of succession.[18] On July 9, 2011, a new country, the Republic of South Sudan, was formed. For the first time in decades, there was a great spirit of hope and joy in South Sudan.

Nevertheless, many challenges remain. There is tension between the North and South marked by outbreaks of violence. Poverty, destruction from war, crumbled infrastructure, tribal conflict, and debates over how to use resources, are immediate concerns. On December 15, 2013, ethnic and political conflict erupted in South Sudan. Tribalism, corruption, the previous war,

---

18 Addario, Lynsey. "World Topics: Sudan" New York Times. 2/8/11 <http://topics.nytimes.com/top/news/countries and territories/sudan/index.html>

arrested development, and continued violence are all root factors in this new challenge to peace. Despite the challenges, South Sudan is still full of hope, promise, and possibilities. It is a beautiful country with ancient theological, technological, philosophical, and artistic traditions. It values community, caring for neighbors, and stewarding the natural world. It is not simply a place of trauma, but a country of strength and innovation, especially in the face of trials and conflict.

The church in Sudan has experienced many changes as well. They have known the joy of revival, but are now confronting a country in upheaval. Now, as much as ever, they are fighting for peace, unity, development, restoration, and redemption. They have lost many leaders and resources. They greatly desire theological education and formation. They need Christian peacemakers to meet the challenges. For these reasons, John remains committed to his vision of raising Christian shepherds throughout South Sudan.

In 2004, John responded to the call on his life and became an Anglican priest. At that time, he founded the Good Shepherd Leadership Training Center in Kakuma Refugee camp to empower lay leaders and Anglican clergy. The demand for his teaching spread all over the refugee camps of East Africa, with over 1,000 students completing his classes.

In 2015 Good Shepherd Leadership Training Center became Good Shepherd College and Seminary and Good Shepherd Academy in Juba, South Sudan. Good Shepherd Academy is a pre-school and primary school that believes in winning young minds at a tender age and training them for the glory of God. These institutions work together to provide theological education to students ages four to twenty-four. Their vision is "molding and nurturing servant leaders in Christian education for the transformation and making of a peaceful society." They provide primary and secondary education to Christians, with certificate courses in Pastoral Care, Counseling, Early Childhood Education, Christian leadership and English language with the hope bringing Christ's redemption to all people.

Good Shepherd College & Seminary, South Sudan (GSCS), formerly known as Good Shepherd Leadership Training Center (GSLTC) started as a mobile training program to empower refugee clergy and lay leaders of the Episcopal Church of Sudan (Anglican). GSCS is dedicated to leadership development, discipleship, teaching and training of leaders in the emerging church of South Sudan, Sudan and beyond. In addition to its Christian leadership development program, GSCS publishes The Christian Times, a newspaper which reports on peace, development, the church in South Sudan, and the work of the college.

John finished his bachelor's degree at Daystar University and was given the opportunity to continue his theological education at Trinity School for Ministry in Ambridge, PA. In 2010, he received a Master of Arts in Religion. John returned home, and in 2012, he met Sarah Alek Daau. They fell deeply in love and were married soon after. Together, they live with and care for his mother, Tabitha, and their sons Jacob, Abraham, and Isaac. He was reunited with his brother, Joseph, who is an accountant. John has hope for the future of South Sudan and looks forward to the day when there will be one Shepherd and one flock.

BIBLIOGRAPHY

Adeyemo, Tokunboh, *Is Africa Cursed? A Vision for the Radical Transformation of An Ailing Continent.* Nairobi: World Alive, 2009.

Barsella, Gino and Guixot, Ayuso Miguel A. *Struggling to Be Heard: The Christian Voice in Independent Sudan 1956 – 1996.* Faith in Sudan No. 4. Nairobi: Paulines, 1998.

Bediako, Kwame. *Jesus in Africa: The Christian Gospel in African History and Experience.* Waynesboro: Paternoster Press, 2004.

Bok, Francis, and Edward Tivnan. *Escape from Slavery: The True Story of My Ten Years in Captivity--and My Journey to Freedom in America.* New York: St. Martin's, 2003.

Denny, Mathewson, Frederick. *An Introduction to Islam.* New York: Macmillian, 1985.

Dinka-Bor Hymnal. Episcopal Church of the Sudan, 1998.

Ela, Jean-Marc. *My Faith As An African.* New York: Orbis, 1988.

Daau, Chol, John. *Personal Interviews.* Nov. 2009 – June, 2010.

Daau, Chol, John. "Good Shepherd in Kakuma." *The New Sudan Christian* (Juba) January-April 2008. Volume 1, Issue No. 9, p. 14.

Hastings, Adrian. *African Christianity.* New York: Seabury, 1976.

Jeske, Christine. *Into the Mud: Inspiration for Everyday Activists.* Chicago: Moody, 2010.

LeMarquand, Grant. "Appropriation of the Cross Among the Jieng People of Southern Sudan." *Journal of Inculturation Theology* 5, no. 2 (2003): 176-98.

LeMarquand, Grant. "An Anglican Perspective on the Future of Anglicanism." Trinity Journal of Theology and Missions 1 (2007), 87.

Marial, Galuak, Samuel. "What is Happening in Sudan? A Prayer Guide for Sudan." Unpublished essay written for Trinity School for Ministry. January, 2011.

Mbiti, John S. *African Religions and Philosophy.* 2nd. rev. ed. Oxford: Heinemann, 1990.

Mugambi, J.N.K. editor, *The Church and The Future in Africa.* Nairobi: All Conferences of Churches, 1997.

Nhial, Abraham, and DiAnn Mills. *Lost Boy No More: A True Story of Survival and Salvation.* Nashville: Broadham and Holman, 2004.

Nikkel, Marc. *The Crosses of The Dinka Christians.* Video. Fox Video Production, 512 Autumn Springs, Suite D, Franklin, TN 37067, www.foxvp.com.

Nikkel, Marc. *Dinka Christianity: The Origins and Development of Christianity Among the Dinka of Sudan with Special Reference to the Songs of Dinka Christians.* Faith in Sudan 11. Nairobi: Paulines, 2001.

Nikkel, Marc. "Jieng 'Songs of Suffering' and the Nature of God." *Anglican and Episcopal History* 71, no. 2 (2002): 223-40.

Nikkel, Marc. *The Outcast, the Stranger, and the Enemy in Dinka Tradition Contrasted with Attitudes of Contemporary Dinka Christians.* Master's Thesis. General Theological Seminary: New York City, 1988.

Nikkel, Marc. Grant LeMarquand, editor. *Why Haven't you Left?: Letters from the Sudan.* New York: Church Publishing Inc., 2

Oden, Thomas C. *How Africa Shaped the Christian Mind.* Downers Grove: InterVarsity, 2007. .

Rhodes, Katie Dr. "Answers to the Cries of My Heart." The New Sudan Christian (Juba) January-April 2008. Volume 1, Issue No. 9, p. 14.
Sanneh, Lamin. *Whose Religion is Christianity? The Gospel Beyond the West.* Grand Rapids: Eerdmans, 2003.
Shorter, Aylward. *African Culture and the Christian Church.* London: Geoffrey Chapman, 1973.
Taryor, Kwiawon Taryor, Sr. *Impact of the African Tradition on African Christianity.* Chicago: Strugglers' Community Press, 1984.
Wanous, Tom and Bette. *Personal Interview.* March 25, 2011.
Wasamu, Moses. "The Role of Church Leaders in South Sudan" *The New Sudan Christian* (Juba) November 23-December 6, 2010. Volume 1, Issue 16, p. 10.
Wasamu, Moses. "Referendum Triggers Exodus" *The New Sudan Christian* (Juba) November 23-December 6, 2010. Volume 1, Issue 16, p. 10.
Werner, Roland, William Anderson, and Andrew C. Wheeler. *Day of Devastation Day of Contentment: the History of the Sudanese Church Across 2000 Years.* Faith in Sudan 10. Nairobi: Paulines Publication, 2000.
Wheeler, Andrew C. and Kayanga, Samuel E. *But God Is Not Defeated: Celebrating the Centenary of the Episcopal Church of the Sudan 1899-1999.* Nairobi: Paulines, 1999.
Wheeler, Andrew C. "A Church of the People: the Role of Sudanese Evangelists." *Announcing the Light: Sudanese Witness to the Gospel.* Faith in Sudan No. 6. Nairobi: Paulines, 1998.
Wheeler, Andrew C. *Land of Promise: Church Growth in a Sudan at War.* Faith in Sudan No. 1. Nairobi: Paulines, 1997.

ABOUT THE AUTHORS

Lilly Sanders Ubbens is an award winning writer, speaker, and teacher. Growing up in San Pedro Sula, Honduras, she has a lifelong love for the diversity of God's people. She holds a master's degree from Trinity School for Ministry. More than this, she is a Christian, wife, and mother. She is married to an Anglican pastor, and they have a ministry in Ocala, Florida.

Rev. John Chol Daau is an ordained Anglican priest, gifted speaker, and preacher. He travels internationally to share his story and plans for the future of South Sudan. He is founder Good Shepherd Academy, Good Shepherd College and Seminary and creator of The Christian Times the leading Christian newspaper in South Sudan.

RECOMMENDED READING

If you are interested in Christ in social Action, please consider Kimberly Rae's India's Street Kids series:

Capturing Jasmina: Capturing Jasmina, fiction for young adult readers by Kimberly Rae, is the story of Jasmina, a young girl in India, and her brother, Samir. The children are sold by their father to a man promising them an education and good jobs. But, as Jasmina and Samir soon discover, the man is providing an education, not in a school, but as a slave in his sweatshop garment factory. While Samir quickly submits to his new life of misery, Jasmina never stops planning an escape. She comes to realize that escape doesn't always mean freedom.

Buying Samir: Set in the world of international child slavery, Buying Samir is the second book in India's Street Kid series by Kimberly Rae. Jasmina dreams of the day when her family will all be reunited. When missionaries Asha and Mark go on summer break, Jasmina leaves safety to search for Samir alone and discovers that her brother is now working for the men that once enslaved them. By attempting to free some girls Samir recruited, Jasmina puts everyone's lives in peril. Has Samir really turned evil? Will he help her get away?

Seeking Mother: "I asked for help, for mercy from the God who sets the captives free."—Jasmina. In Seeking Mother, the third book in the India's Street Kids Series, Jasmina joins Amrita in a dangerous plan to bring down a human trafficking ring in Kolkata. Getting a lead on the location of her parents, Jasmina enlists the help of a new friend to find them. When she finally crosses paths with Samir again, she starts to question who she can trust.

If you would like to grow closer to God through devotions, please consider these devotionals from Hartline:

Chaim Bentorah's *Hebrew Word Study: Ancient Biblical Words Put into a Modern Context with the Help of the People Who Ride My Bus:* Hebrew Word Study Ancient Biblical Words Put Into A Modern Context is different from other Hebrew word study books as this book takes a specific passage of Scripture and analyzes it with respect to its historical and cultural background. It takes key Hebrew words in this passage of Scripture and drills down to the very heart, soul and core of the Hebrew word and where appropriate traces that word to its Semitic origins. This is then put into a devotional format using the author's experiences from driving a disability bus to help illustrate and put these Scriptures and Hebrew words into a modern context for every day Christian living.

Chaim Bentorah's *God's Love for Us:* Built on the premise that God created the marriage relationship as a model of our relationship with Him, God's Love for Us explores the possibility that being created in the image of God means we were given a heart like God. Through the Biblical understanding of a marriage relationship between a man and woman, we begin to understand how the love, intimacy, caring, nurturing, security and dependency that we find in our natural marriage relationship is meant to help us relate to our salvation and consequential bonding with the God of the universe.

Mary Selzer's *Wait a Minute!:* In our lifetimes we will live millions of moments. Each one is an experience. Experiences turn into lessons, and lessons become legacies. In Wait A Minute! the author takes a fresh look at everyday happenings and draws from scripture to leave readers with the challenge to discover those specific times in life where learning is obvious but the lesson might be missed. These thirty devotionals are unique, thoughtful and encouraging.

Marilyn Turk's *Lighthouse Devotions:* Lighthouses—inspiring symbols of hope, refuge, safety, security, and strength. People the world over are drawn to them and what they represent. Every continent has at least one lighthouse guarding its shores, warning mariners of danger and showing them where they are. God's Word does the same for everyone. Yet it not only provides daily guidance but also eternal direction for safety and well-being. It is no surprise, then, that God used the term "light" to represent what He and His Word are to mankind. *Lighthouse Devotions* are stories about real lighthouses and people who lived in them, and how these stories demonstrate biblical principles found in God's Word.